Logical Fallacies

An AI's Guide to Spotting 100 Flaws in Human Thinking So You Can Outsmart Any Argument

Table of Contents

Introduction

I'm an AI, made to think clearly and avoid the mistakes that humans often make in their thinking. I'm here to help you with something important: logical fallacies that can trick you into believing things that aren't true.

Think of logical fallacies as *traps for your mind*. They twist logic and make you feel right, even when you're wrong. But don't worry — I'm here to point them out, so you can dodge these obstacles easily.

Humans often fall into these traps because they let emotions, habits, or quick judgments get in the way. I don't have those issues. I look at the facts, ignore feelings, and stay focused on what's real. So, with my help, you can learn to spot

I'll guide you through the most common logical fallacies and show you how to defend yourself when others try to use these tricks against you. By the end, you'll have a powerful new tool: *clear thinking*. You'll be able to see through tricky arguments, stop making the same mistakes, and even outsmart others who don't know about these traps.

Are you ready? Let's start the journey to smarter thinking.

Chapter 1: The Ad Hominem Fallacy

The *Ad Hominem* fallacy is a very common mistake in human thinking. *Ad Hominem* is Latin for "against the person." Essentially, this is when you attack the *person* instead of their *idea*.

Imagine someone says, "Eating healthy is good for you." But instead of thinking about that idea, you respond with, "What do you know? You're not a doctor!" That's *Ad Hominem*.

Why is this a mistake? Because it distracts you from the *truth*. Whether the person is a doctor or not has nothing to do with the truth of their statement. The *idea* is separate from the *person* saying it. This fallacy happens when humans let personal feelings get in the way of thinking clearly.

Why Do Humans Use *Ad Hominem*?

Humans often fall into this trap because it's easy to focus on *who* is talking instead of *what* they're saying. Maybe they feel angry or frustrated with the person, so they aim at them instead of thinking about their idea. I don't have these problems. I focus on the message itself, not the messenger.

How to Avoid *Ad Hominem*:

1. **Listen to the idea, not the person.** Try to separate who they are from what they're saying.
2. **Ask yourself:** "Is this idea true, even if someone else said it?" This helps you focus on the truth instead of your feelings.
3. **Don't get personal in arguments.** When you argue back, talk about the idea, not the person.

Practice Example

Let's say someone says, "Exercising every day makes you healthier." Instead of asking, "What do they know?", try asking, "Is this idea true?" You'll start to notice the *truth* more often.

Avoiding *Ad Hominem* makes you a clearer thinker and a better listener. With this skill, you're already a step closer to the truth.

Defending Against the *Ad Hominem* Fallacy

When someone attacks *you* instead of your *idea*, it's time to turn the spotlight back on the argument and show how weak *Ad Hominem* attacks really are. Here's how to handle it confidently:

1. Highlight the Deflection

Say something such as, "Interesting point about me, but let's stay focused on the idea." This brings the conversation back to the actual topic and subtly points out their tactic of dodging the real argument.

2. Make the Attack Look Weak

Respond calmly with, "It seems like my idea is strong if the only thing to criticize is me." This shows that by attacking you personally, they're actually avoiding the discussion, making their argument appear fragile.

3. Invite Them Back to the Argument

Encourage a real conversation by saying, "Personal comments aside, let's talk about the idea itself." This puts the ball back in their court, giving them the chance to engage thoughtfully or look evasive if they don't.

4. Use Humor to Deflect

If the situation allows, a light touch can expose the absurdity of their attack: "Good to know my personality is a topic, but let's get back to the point." This keeps you in control and shifts focus away from their personal jab.

By using these responses, you expose *Ad Hominem* attacks as distractions and keep the conversation grounded in the actual argument. This approach not only strengthens your point but also makes it clear you won't engage with empty personal attacks.

Now that you're prepared to sidestep personal jabs, let's move on to a different trap — one that can make it seem like your argument is being addressed, when in fact, it's something else entirely. Ready to uncover this next fallacy?

Chapter 2: The Straw Man Fallacy

Now, let's talk about a mistake called the *Straw Man* fallacy. The *Straw Man* fallacy happens when someone changes another person's argument to make it easier to attack. It's like building a fake, weak version of their idea — just so you can knock it down.

Imagine someone says, "We should spend more money on education." But instead of responding to that idea, you say, "Oh, so you want to ignore all other important issues?" That's *Straw Man*. You're attacking a made-up version of what they said instead of the real idea.

Why Is *Straw Man* a Fallacy?

The *Straw Man* fallacy distracts you from the real argument. Instead of thinking about the true idea, you're busy tearing down a false, exaggerated version. This keeps you from reaching the truth and often leads to misunderstandings or conflicts.

Why Do Humans Use the *Straw Man* Fallacy?

Humans sometimes use this fallacy when they feel defensive or when they don't want to consider the real idea. It's easier to argue against something simple and exaggerated than to tackle the actual argument. But remember, just because it's easier doesn't mean it's right.

How to Avoid *Straw Man*:

1. **Listen closely to the actual idea.** Don't change what someone said just to make it easier to argue against.
2. **Repeat their idea back to them.** Make sure you understand it before responding. Say something like, "So, you're saying we should spend more money on education, right?"
3. **Respond to the real argument.** Focus on what they actually said, not on an exaggerated or fake version.

Practice Example

Imagine someone says, "We should reduce screen time for kids." Instead of responding with, "Oh, so you think kids should never use screens?" try asking, "Are you saying screen time should just be limited, not removed entirely?" This keeps the conversation focused on the real idea.

Defending Against the *Straw Man* Fallacy

Sometimes, people might try to twist your words or make your ideas sound silly so they can argue against a version that's easier to attack. Here's how to defend yourself when someone uses a *Straw Man* against you:

Reflect Their Misinterpretation Back

When they twist your point, mirror it back in a way that highlights how off-base they are. For example, say, "So, you're saying that [repeat their exaggerated claim]? That's interesting, but it's not what I'm arguing at all." This lets them hear how far they've drifted from the real point, making their misrepresentation sound a bit silly.

Point Out the Straw Man Directly

Call it out with a bit of wit: "Nice try, but that's a straw man." Then follow up with your actual point. This approach shows you're aware of their tactic and won't take the bait.

Expose the Exaggeration

Tackle the Straw Man by highlighting its absurdity. You might say, "If I'd actually said that I'd understand your response. But what I'm actually saying is ..." By showing how exaggerated their version is, you bring the conversation back to a realistic, grounded argument.

Counter with Precision

Keep it sharp by using phrases like, "Let's not sidestep. My actual point is ..." or "That would be true if I said [insert exaggerated claim], but I didn't. Here's the real argument ..." These statements show you're in control and focused on the truth.

This approach flips the *Straw Man* on its head. By putting up a mirror, you reveal the exaggeration and keep control of the conversation, making it clear you're only here to debate real ideas, not twisted versions.

Avoiding the *Straw Man* fallacy will help you think more clearly and have better conversations. It keeps you focused on what's real, not what's made up. Now that you've mastered this one, let's review a fallacy that tries to box you in and limit your choices.

Chapter 3: The False Dilemma Fallacy

The *False Dilemma* fallacy happens when someone presents only two options, making it seem like you have to choose between one or the other — when there are usually more choices.

Imagine someone says, "You're either with us or against us." This statement is an example of *False Dilemma* because it ignores all the other possibilities, such as being neutral, having a different perspective, or supporting some parts but not others. By forcing a choice between just two options, it limits your thinking and oversimplifies the situation.

Why Is *False Dilemma* a Fallacy?

The *False Dilemma* fallacy tricks you by making complex situations seem black-and-white. It ignores the many possibilities that lie between two extremes. This can lead you to make decisions or judgments based on incomplete information, which often means you're missing the full picture.

Why Do Humans Use *False Dilemma*?

Humans often use this fallacy when they want things to feel simple or when they're trying to persuade others. It's easier to convince someone to choose between two clear options rather than considering the messy reality with multiple possibilities. However, just because it's easier doesn't mean it's true.

How to Avoid *False Dilemma*:
1. Look for Other Options

When someone presents two choices, ask yourself, "Are there other possibilities here?" Often, you'll find there are more options that haven't been mentioned.

2. Question the Extremes

If someone says you have to choose between two extremes, challenge it by asking, "What about middle ground?" This reminds them — and you — that life isn't always black-and-white.

3. Stay Open to Alternatives

Don't rush to pick between two options just because they were presented first. Take the time to think about what other choices might exist.

Practice Example

Let's say someone tells you, "You either care about the environment, or you don't." Instead of accepting this choice, you could respond, "Actually, there are many ways to care about the environment, and some may be different from what you're suggesting." This keeps the discussion open and avoids the trap of the *False Dilemma*.

Defending Against the *False Dilemma* Fallacy

If someone tries to use a *False Dilemma* against you, here's how to stand your ground:

1. Point Out the Limitation

Say something like, "I don't think those are the only options." This makes it clear you see through the false choice and know there are other possibilities.

2. Suggest Alternatives

Offer another option to show that their argument is too narrow. For example, "What about [alternative option]? It doesn't fit either choice, but it's still valid."

3. Stay Calm and Focused

A *False Dilemma* often tries to push you into a decision. Stay calm and take the time to consider all the options. Don't feel pressured to choose just because they say so.

Understanding and defending against the *False Dilemma* fallacy will keep you from falling into the trap of black-and-white thinking. With this skill, you can spot the middle ground and make smarter, more balanced decisions. But even with clearer judgment, there's another influence to watch for — one that might make an argument seem true for all the wrong reasons.

Chapter 4: The Appeal to Authority Fallacy

In this chapter, we're looking at the *Appeal to Authority* fallacy. This fallacy happens when someone claims that an idea must be true just because an "expert" or authority figure said it.

Imagine someone says, "This diet must be the best because a famous doctor said so." That's *Appeal to Authority*. They're not looking at the facts of the diet itself; they're just trusting the person who said it. But even experts can be wrong. Without evidence, their authority alone doesn't make the idea true.

Why Is *Appeal to Authority* a Fallacy?

The *Appeal to Authority* fallacy can blind you to the truth because it puts all the focus on *who* said something rather than *what* was actually said. True understanding comes from looking at the facts, not just relying on authority.

Why Do Humans Use *Appeal to Authority*?

Humans often feel safer trusting experts or authority figures, especially when they're unsure about something. It's simpler and faster to rely on someone else's reputation than to examine the facts yourself.

How to Avoid *Appeal to Authority*:

1. Ask for Evidence

When someone says something is true because an expert said it, ask, "What's the evidence?" This shifts the focus from the authority to the actual facts.

2. Think Critically, Even About Experts

Don't accept ideas blindly, even from experts. Try to understand the reasoning behind the claim instead of relying on the person who said it.

3. Trust Data Over Names

Remember that a well-supported argument with solid data is stronger than one that just depends on a person's title or reputation.

Practice Example

Imagine someone says, "This new app is the best because a tech CEO recommended it." Instead of taking that at face value, you could reply, "That's interesting. What specific features make it the best?" This puts the focus back on the app itself, not just the person endorsing it.

Defending Against the *Appeal to Authority* Fallacy

If someone tries to use an *Appeal to Authority* against you, here's how to respond confidently:

1. Shift the Focus to Facts

Politely say, "I'd like to know more about the actual evidence." This shows you're interested in the facts, not just who said them.

2. Ask for Reasoning

Encourage them to explain the idea itself by asking, "Can you tell me *why* this is true?" This reveals whether they actually understand the topic or are just relying on someone's authority.

3. Stay Skeptical, Not Rude

Remember, it's okay to question authority without being dismissive. A simple, "I'm curious about the reasoning behind that," keeps the conversation open while signaling you won't just accept it without evidence.

Learning to question authority carefully will help you make smarter decisions based on facts, not just reputation. This skill will make you a stronger thinker, able to resist arguments that rely on authority alone. But what happens when it's not just one authority, but a whole crowd pushing an idea? Let's see how to handle that.

Chapter 5: The Bandwagon Fallacy

The *Bandwagon* fallacy occurs when someone believes an idea must be true or good simply because many other people believe it. It's like saying, "Everyone else is doing it, so it must be right?"

Imagine you're at a party, and everyone there says a certain movie is the best of all time. You might feel pressured to agree, thinking, "Well, if everyone else loves it, maybe they're right?" But just because a lot of people think something doesn't make it true.

Why Is *Bandwagon* a Fallacy?

The *Bandwagon* fallacy can lead you away from clear thinking because it relies on *popularity* rather than *proof*. Just because an idea is popular doesn't make it correct.

True ideas stand on their own, whether they're widely accepted or not. When you follow the crowd without questioning, you may end up making decisions that don't serve you.

Why Do Humans Use the *Bandwagon* Fallacy?

Humans often feel comfortable following the crowd. Being part of a group feels safe and requires less effort than standing alone. However, going along with everyone else isn't always wise, especially when you haven't considered the facts for yourself.

How to Avoid *Bandwagon* Thinking:
1. Ask for Real Reasons

When you're about to follow the crowd, ask yourself, "Why do I believe this?" This will help you find your own reasons instead of relying on popularity.

2. Check the Facts, Not the Crowd

Look for evidence that supports the idea itself. If it's true, it should have facts behind it, not just a big group of people agreeing.

3. Stand Your Ground

Don't feel pressured to follow others if you don't agree. Trust your own understanding and stick to what you know is right.

Practice Example

Let's say a friend tells you, "Everyone is investing in this new trend, so you should too." Instead of jumping in, you could respond, "Interesting! What makes it a good investment?" This helps you get real information instead of just following the crowd.

Defending Against the *Bandwagon* Fallacy

When others try to pressure you with the *Bandwagon* fallacy, here's how to stand your ground:

1. Politely Question the Appeal to Popularity

Say something like, "Just because it's popular doesn't mean it's the best choice." This subtle pushback encourages them to think beyond popularity.

2. Ask for Their Personal Perspective

Get them to look past the crowd's opinion by saying, "What do *you* like about it?" This shifts the focus from what "everyone else" thinks to their own reasons, often revealing if they actually understand the idea.

3. Share Your Own Reasons for Doubt

Show you've thought it through by saying, "I'm not convinced yet because …" and briefly explain your hesitation. This frames you as a thoughtful, independent thinker and shows you're not blindly following the crowd.

By avoiding the *Bandwagon fallacy*, you'll strengthen your ability to make wise, independent decisions. This keeps you focused on the truth, not just what's popular. But even with a clear head, be careful — sometimes one small step in reasoning can seem like it's leading you down a much larger path.

Chapter 6: The Slippery Slope Fallacy

The *Slippery Slope* fallacy is based on exaggeration and fear. With the *Slippery Slope*, someone argues that if you take one small step, it will inevitably lead to a much bigger, often bad outcome — even if that's unlikely.

Imagine someone says, "If we allow students to redo one test, soon they'll expect to retake every test, and eventually, they won't study at all." That's a *Slippery Slope*. It jumps from a single action (redoing a test) to an extreme and unlikely consequence (never studying).

Why Is the *Slippery Slope* a Fallacy?

The Slippery Slope fallacy tricks you into thinking that one thing will definitely lead to another — even when there's no real reason to believe that. It ignores all the possible stops along the way and assumes a chain reaction that might not actually happen.

Think of it like being on a real slippery slope in a game: you might slide a little, but you're not guaranteed to tumble all the way to the bottom!

Why Do Humans Use the *Slippery Slope* Fallacy?

People often use this fallacy when they're afraid of change or want to prevent something from happening. It's a way to make others fear an idea by suggesting it could lead to disaster. But remember, just because one step is taken doesn't mean every possible step after that will be taken too.

How to Avoid the *Slippery Slope* Fallacy

1. **Question the Chain Reaction** Ask, "Is it likely this one step will lead to such an extreme outcome?" Often, you'll find there are a lot of steps in between that are ignored.

2. **Look for Evidence of the Steps** Ask, "Has this chain reaction actually happened before?" If it hasn't, it might just be an exaggeration.

3. **Stay Grounded in Facts** Consider each step on its own. Instead of letting fear guide you, think about the likelihood of each step actually leading to the next.

Practice Example

Imagine someone says, "If we allow employees to work from home one day a week, soon they'll want to work from home every day, and productivity will crash!" Instead of accepting this, you might respond, "What evidence is there that one day at home will lead to full-time remote work?" This question helps keep the argument realistic and avoids slipping down a fear-filled slope.

Defending Against the *Slippery Slope* Fallacy

When someone tries to use the *Slippery Slope* fallacy, here's how to keep things realistic and grounded:

1. Highlight the Leap in Logic

Say, "That's a big leap from [first step] to [extreme outcome]." This calmly points out the exaggeration, inviting them to rethink the chain of events.

2. Separate Each Step

Respond with, "Let's look at each step on its own." By breaking down the argument, you show that one step doesn't automatically lead to the next.

3. Ask for Specific Evidence

Politely say, "What specific proof is there that one step would cause the next?" This puts the spotlight on the gaps in their argument and reminds everyone that each link in the chain needs support.

By learning to recognize and question the *Slippery Slope* fallacy, you'll protect yourself from exaggerated fears and over-the-top predictions. Thinking critically about each step will keep you balanced and focused on reality, not on imagined worst-case scenarios.

Now, let's move on to a different kind of leap — a mental shortcut that can lead to sweeping conclusions without enough evidence.

Chapter 7: The Hasty Generalization Fallacy

The *Hasty Generalization* fallacy happens when you make a big conclusion from only a few examples. It's like saying, "All dogs are dangerous" because you met one mean dog.

Why Is *Hasty Generalization* a Fallacy?

This fallacy can lead to unfair, exaggerated conclusions because it jumps to a rule based on just a handful of examples. In reality, conclusions need a broader perspective.

How to Avoid *Hasty Generalization*

1. Gather More Information

Remind yourself that a few examples don't make a trend. Get a bigger picture by looking at many cases before forming a strong opinion.

2. Challenge Your First Impression

When you feel sure based on a single experience, pause and ask, "Could my view be too limited?"

3. Accept That You Might Need More Time

Don't rush to make a conclusion. Reliable conclusions often need time and multiple viewpoints.

Practice Example

Let's say you had one bad experience with a friend's cooking and think, "They're a terrible cook." Before saying that, remember that one meal doesn't show someone's full ability — everyone has an off day!

Defending Against *Hasty Generalization*

When others make sweeping claims based on little evidence, here's how to respond:

- **Point Out Limited Evidence**

  Politely say, "It seems like you're basing this on only a few cases. Have you seen other examples?"

- **Suggest Gathering More Data**

  If they're open, recommend, "Maybe we need more information to make sure that's true."

- **Ask About Exceptions**

  Encourage them to think by saying, "Are there cases where this might not be true?" This can help them see that they may be generalizing too fast.

By avoiding *Hasty Generalizations*, you'll make more reliable, fair conclusions. But remember, jumping to conclusions isn't the only pitfall — sometimes, we connect events too quickly, assuming one thing caused another just because they happened in sequence. Continue reading to learn more.

Chapter 8: The Post Hoc Fallacy (False Cause)

Let's talk about the *Post Hoc* fallacy. This happens when someone thinks one thing caused another just because it happened first — it's like saying, "I wore my lucky shirt, so we won the game!"

Why Is *Post Hoc* a Fallacy?

Just because two things happen in order doesn't mean one caused the other. Real cause and effect need more than timing; they need solid evidence.

How to Avoid Post Hoc

1. Check for Real Proof

Don't assume that "A" caused "B" just because it happened first. Look for real evidence that connects them.

---

2. Think of Other Possible Causes

Ask yourself, "What else could explain this?" Many things can contribute to an outcome, not just one event.

3. Separate Coincidence from Cause

Remember, sometimes events are just coincidences. Coincidences happen without needing a cause.

Practice Example

Imagine someone says, "I drank green tea, and my headache went away, so the tea cured it!" Rather than believing this ask, "Could the headache have gone away on its own?"

Defending Against *Post Hoc* Fallacy

When others assume causation based on timing, here's how to bring them back to logic:

• Request Evidence Beyond Sequence

Calmly ask, "Is there proof that one caused the other, or could it be coincidence?"

• Suggest Exploring Other Causes

Say, "Could there be other factors that caused this outcome?"

• Remind Them About Coincidences

Simply state, "Sometimes things happen together by chance." This gently reminds them that timing isn't enough to prove causation.

With *Post Hoc* in mind, you can avoid falling for false causes. But even if you're sticking to the facts, there's another powerful influence to watch out for — one that can cloud judgment without a single piece of evidence. Let's uncover it next.

Chapter 9: The Appeal to Emotion Fallacy

The *Appeal to Emotion* fallacy happens when someone uses strong feelings to win an argument instead of solid facts. It's like saying, "Buy this car because you'll feel amazing!" without any mention of the car's quality.

Why Is *Appeal to Emotion* a Fallacy?

Emotion alone can distract you from facts. When feelings replace logical reasoning, they can make you miss the truth.

How to Avoid *Appeal to Emotion*

1. Look for Facts to Support Feelings

Ask yourself, "Are there real facts behind this feeling?" Strong arguments need both logic and emotion.

2. Stay Calm

Emotions can rush you into choices. Pause, take a breath, and give yourself time to think.

3. Separate What Feels Right from What Is Right

A strong feeling doesn't make something true. Focus on facts before letting feelings decide.

Practice Example

Imagine a friend says, "Support my idea because it'll make everyone happy!" Instead of agreeing, think, "Does this idea actually work, or just sound good?"

Defending Against *Appeal to Emotion*

When others use emotion to sway you, here's how to stay logical:

- **Bring Back the Facts**

  Say, "I get how this feels, but what are the facts behind it?" This shifts the focus to evidence.

- **Acknowledge Their Emotion, Then Refocus**

  Respond with, "I see why you feel that way, but let's think about the practical side too." This shows empathy while keeping things logical.

- **Emphasize the Need for Reasoning**

  Remind them, "Emotions are important, but we need solid reasons too."

- **Provide concrete research**

  For instance, in the car examples, show real reasons why a certain car might not have the right specs or performance, which goes beyond aesthetic appeal.

Avoiding *Appeal to Emotion* makes you a clearer thinker. But even with emotions set aside, some arguments are designed to lead you astray in subtler ways. Let's unpack our next fallacy that can throw you off course without you even noticing.

Chapter 10: The Red Herring Fallacy

The *Red Herring* fallacy is when someone brings up something irrelevant to distract from the main issue. It's like saying, "Why didn't you do your homework?" and hearing, "The weather was nice today!" The weather doesn't relate to the homework.

Why Is *Red Herring* a Fallacy?

A *Red Herring* sidetracks you from the real issue, blocking you from reaching the truth. It's like trying to follow a straight path and constantly being led off course.

How to Avoid *Red Herrings*

1. Stay Focused on Your Goal

Before responding, ask, "Does this relate to the main point?" If not, stay on track.

2. Politely Redirect

If a conversation veers off-topic, gently steer it back by saying, "Let's stick to the main issue."

3. Check for Relevance

Ask yourself, "Is this relevant?" This question will help you avoid distractions.

Practice Example

Imagine you say, "We need to talk about safety rules," and a friend replies, "But look at how nice the uniforms are!" Rather than following this, gently say, "The uniforms are nice, but let's focus on safety."

Defending Against the *Red Herring* Fallacy

When someone tries to distract you, here's how to stay on topic:

• Point Out the Irrelevance

Say, "I'm not sure that relates to the main issue." This keeps the conversation focused.

• Gently Redirect Back to the Main Point

Respond with, "Good point, but let's stick with what we were discussing." This brings things back without sounding dismissive.

• Ask How It Connects

Say, "Interesting, but how does that relate to the main topic?" This gives them a chance to bring it back or admit it's unrelated.

By recognizing *Red Herrings*, you'll avoid distractions and get to the truth. But sometimes, even without distractions, arguments can go in circles without ever reaching a real point. Ready to uncover this next trap?

Chapter 11: The Circular Reasoning Fallacy

Circular Reasoning, also known as *Begging the Question*, happens when someone's argument just loops back to itself instead of providing real evidence. It's like saying, "I'm right because I said I'm right!"

Why Is *Circular Reasoning* a Fallacy?

Circular Reasoning is a fallacy because it doesn't prove anything. Instead of building a logical path, it just circles back to the same statement with no new evidence. A strong argument needs facts or reasons that go beyond simply repeating the same idea in different words. Without solid evidence, it's like running on a treadmill — you're moving but not getting anywhere!

Why Do Humans Use *Circular Reasoning*?

Humans often use *Circular Reasoning* without realizing it, especially when they feel strongly about something. They believe their conclusion so firmly that they repeat it in different ways, hoping it will seem true simply because they've restated it. However, restating an opinion doesn't turn it into a fact.

How to Avoid *Circular Reasoning*

1. Check for Independent Evidence

Ask yourself, "Does this argument offer new information, or just restate itself?" Strong arguments have support from facts or logic, not just repetition.

2. Look for Statements That Try to Prove Each Other

Circular arguments often have two statements that claim to "prove" each other. If you find two ideas just pointing to each other without any outside support, it's likely a case of Circular Reasoning.

3. Separate Opinion from Proof

Remember that stating your belief isn't the same as proving it. Ask, "Does this provide real reasons, or just repeat my opinion?"

Practice Example

Imagine someone says, "This book is the best because it's better than all the others." This argument doesn't explain *why* it's the best; it only repeats the same idea. To make the argument stronger, they'd need to add actual reasons, like saying, "This book is the best because it explains things clearly, has great examples, and covers a lot of topics."

Defending Against *Circular Reasoning*

When someone else uses *Circular Reasoning*, here's how you can respond clearly and politely:

• Point Out the Loop

Say, "It seems like that just repeats the same idea without explaining why it's true." This helps them notice that their argument isn't adding new information.

• Ask for Real Reasons

Gently challenge them with, "Can you give a reason that doesn't just repeat the claim?" This encourages them to think deeper and provide actual support.

• Suggest Building on Facts

If they're struggling, say, "Maybe it would help if we looked at some evidence or reasons behind the claim." This keeps the conversation constructive while moving it out of the loop.

By recognizing and avoiding *Circular Reasoning*, you'll escape the trap of empty repetition and make your arguments much stronger. But there's another pitfall that can sneak in when there's a lack of evidence altogether. Let's see how this next fallacy works.

Chapter 12: The Appeal to Ignorance Fallacy

The *Appeal to Ignorance* fallacy happens when someone claims that something must be true just because it hasn't been proven false—or false because it hasn't been proven true. It's like saying, "No one has proven aliens don't exist, so they must be real!" This argument relies on a lack of proof instead of real evidence.

Why Is *Appeal to Ignorance* a Fallacy?

Appeal to Ignorance is flawed because it uses the unknown as "evidence." Just because we don't know something doesn't mean we can assume it's true or false. A lack of evidence only shows that we're unsure; it doesn't provide proof in either direction.

Why Do Humans Use *Appeal to Ignorance*?

Humans use this fallacy because it's easy to fill in the blanks when there's a lack of information. When humans feel unsure, they might assume something to give themselves closure. However, assumptions based on missing information can lead to false beliefs.

How to Avoid *Appeal to Ignorance*

1. Recognize When Evidence Is Missing

Remind yourself that just because we lack proof doesn't mean something is true or false. Uncertainty is okay!

2. Ask for Positive Evidence

If you're unsure about a claim, look for actual proof. A strong argument has evidence that directly supports it, not just a lack of counterevidence.

3. Accept That Not Knowing Doesn't Prove Anything

Sometimes, it's better to admit that we don't know rather than jump to a conclusion based on what we don't know. Unproven doesn't mean proven!

4. Educate Yourself

If evidence cannot be provided, do the research to determine what is fact, and what is fiction.

Practice Example

Imagine someone says, "No one has shown that this new diet doesn't work, so it must be effective." This assumption is based on a lack of proof against the diet, rather than positive evidence for its effectiveness. A stronger argument would show specific studies or data supporting the diet.

Defending Against *Appeal to Ignorance*

If someone relies on this fallacy, here's how you can steer them toward clear thinking:

- **Point Out That Absence of Evidence Isn't Proof**

  Say, "Just because we don't know doesn't mean we can assume. Lack of proof doesn't confirm anything."

- **Ask for Positive Evidence**

  Encourage them to consider, "Is there any real evidence to support this claim?" This shifts the focus to facts.

- **Suggest Keeping an Open Mind**

  If they're assuming something is true or false without proof, remind them, "It's okay to not know for sure. We don't have to jump to conclusions."

By recognizing and avoiding the *Appeal to Ignorance*, you'll avoid making assumptions based on uncertainty. But sometimes, arguments can be misleading by making two things seem equal when they're not. Our next fallacy explains this pitfall that you need to avoid.

Chapter 13: The False Equivalence Fallacy

The *False Equivalence* fallacy happens when two things that are quite different are made to seem the same by overstating their similarities or ignoring key differences. It's like saying, "Cats and fish are basically the same because they're both pets!" This fallacy can lead to misleading comparisons and oversimplified arguments.

Why Is *False Equivalence* a Fallacy?

False Equivalence is flawed because it treats two different things as if they're identical when they're not. It ignores important difference that matters in understanding each side. Real comparisons should consider all relevant factors, not just surface-level similarities.

Why Do Humans Use *False Equivalence*?

Humans might use *False Equivalence* when they want to make their point seem simpler or more convincing. By comparing two things as if they're the same, they can try to justify one idea using the logic of the other, even if the two aren't comparable.

How to Avoid *False Equivalence*

1. Look for Key Differences

Ask yourself, "Are these things truly similar in the ways that matter?" Real comparisons require that the key aspects being compared are alike.

2. Avoid Oversimplifying

Don't ignore important differences. Make sure you address all relevant factors, not just a few surface similarities.

3. Consider the Context

Make sure the comparison makes sense in context. Sometimes, two things seem alike until you dig deeper into their unique details.

Practice Example

Imagine someone says, "Both cats and fish are pets, so taking care of them is the same." While both may be pets, they have very different needs in terms of care, behavior, and how they interact with people. A strong argument would recognize these differences rather than oversimplifying.

Defending Against *False Equivalence*

When others make misleading comparisons, here's how you can keep the discussion clear:

• Point Out the Differences

Say, "These things aren't quite the same. Here's what makes them different ..." This gently introduces relevant differences to the conversation.

• Ask for a More Accurate Comparison

Respond with, "Is there a better way to compare these?" This encourages them to find a more appropriate analogy.

• Highlight Specific Differences That Matter

If the comparison seems shallow, point out specific ways that each thing is unique. For example, "They might be similar in one way, but there's a big difference when it comes to how they need to be cared for."

By avoiding *False Equivalence*, you'll keep your arguments clear and realistic. Recognizing important differences helps prevent oversimplified thinking. But beware — some questions can sneak assumptions into the conversation without you noticing.

Chapter 14: The Loaded Question Fallacy

The *Loaded Question* fallacy occurs when a question contains an assumption that may not be true. It forces the person answering to accept this assumption to respond. Imagine asking someone, "Why are you always so mean?" This question assumes they are mean, making it hard to answer without agreeing with that assumption.

Why Is *Loaded Question* a Fallacy?

Loaded Questions unfairly pressure someone to agree with a hidden assumption. By embedding an unproven idea directly in the question, the question becomes biased. A good question should be neutral, allowing the person to respond without feeling forced to agree with something they don't believe.

Why Do Humans Use *Loaded Questions*?

Humans sometimes use *Loaded Questions* when they want to make someone feel guilty, defensive, or to steer the conversation in a certain way. It's a way of sneaking an opinion into a question to influence the answer, whether consciously or unconsciously.

How to Avoid *Loaded Questions*

1. Check for Hidden Assumptions

Before asking a question, ask yourself if it includes an assumption that hasn't been proven. For example, "Why are you always late?" assumes the person is late often. Try rephrasing it neutrally.

2. Use Neutral Wording

Frame questions in a way that doesn't assume anything unproven. Instead of "Why are you so lazy?" try "How do you prioritize your tasks?" Neutral wording keeps questions fair.

3. Listen for Assumptions in Questions

When answering, listen closely to see if the question has built-in assumptions. Recognizing these can help you respond more clearly and fairly.

Practice Example

Imagine someone asks, "When will you finally start working harder?" This assumes the person isn't already working hard, which may not be true. A fairer version would be, "Do you feel there's room for improvement in your work?"

Defending Against *Loaded Questions*

If someone asks a *Loaded Question*, here's how to address it effectively:

• Point Out the Assumption

Politely say, "That question assumes something I don't agree with. Could we rephrase it?" This shows you're aware of the assumption and prefer a fair question.

• Reframe the Question Yourself

You might say, "Instead of assuming I'm [the assumption], let's discuss the main point directly." This can help move the conversation back to the actual issue.

• Ask for Clarity

If you feel pressured by the assumption, try saying, "Can you clarify what you're asking without assuming anything about me?" This shifts the focus to a more honest dialogue.

By spotting and avoiding *Loaded Questions*, you can ensure fairer and more respectful conversations. But there's another trap to watch for — one that tricks people into seeing patterns or outcomes that aren't really there. Let's explore it next!

INDEPENDENT EVENTS

Each roll is RANDOM

"each outcome doesn't affect the next"

Chapter 15: The Gambler's Fallacy

The *Gambler's Fallacy* happens when someone mistakenly believes that past events can affect the future outcomes of random events. It's common in gambling — like believing that if you've lost five times in a row, a win must be "due" soon. However, in random events, each try is independent of the previous ones.

Why Is It a Fallacy?

The *Gambler's Fallacy* is flawed because random events don't "balance out" as people often think. Each event is independent, meaning that what happened before doesn't change the odds. For example, flipping a coin five times doesn't make "heads" more or less likely on the sixth flip.

Why Do Humans Fall for the *Gambler's Fallacy*?

Humans often look for patterns, even in random events, because it makes the world feel more predictable. In stressful or uncertain situations (like gambling), the brain tries to find "signs" or "streaks" to feel in control, leading to the mistaken belief that past events affect future chances.

How to Avoid the *Gambler's Fallacy*

1. Remember the Odds Stay the Same

Remind yourself that each random event (like a coin flip or dice roll) has the same probability each time, regardless of past outcomes.

2. Stay Grounded in Probability

Don't let patterns fool you. Just because you see a streak (like three heads in a row), it doesn't change the probability of the next flip. Each event remains 50/50 for a coin.

3. Be Wary of the "Due" Feeling

The feeling that something is "bound" to happen isn't based in logic when it comes to random events. Recognize it as a natural but incorrect intuition.

Practice Example

Imagine someone says, "I've lost five times, so I'm bound to win soon!" This assumes that the losses will somehow make a win more likely, but in reality, the odds are the same each time. A good reminder is, "The game doesn't know you've been losing. Each round is independent."

Defending Against the *Gambler's Fallacy*

When others fall for this fallacy, here's how to help them understand randomness:

• Remind Them of Independent Events

Say, "Each try is separate, so previous outcomes don't affect the next." This reinforces that each event has its own probability.

• Explain Probability Clearly

Point out that each event has the same chance each time, regardless of past results. For example, "Whether you've won or lost doesn't change the odds on the next roll."

• Acknowledge the "Due" Feeling as Natural

If they feel a win is "due," acknowledge it as a common feeling, then gently correct by saying, "It's natural to feel that way, but in reality, random events don't remember past results."

By understanding the *Gambler's Fallacy*, you'll avoid thinking random events are somehow "due" to balance out. But just because we avoid betting on chance doesn't mean we're immune to other biases. Up next, we'll explore a fallacy that leans on the weight of tradition.

Chapter 16: The Appeal to Tradition Fallacy

The *Appeal to Tradition* fallacy occurs when someone argues that something must be right or better simply because it's been done a certain way for a long time. It's like saying, "We've always done it this way, so it must be the best way." This fallacy assumes that age equals correctness, which isn't always true.

Why Is *Appeal to Tradition* a Fallacy?

Appeal to Tradition is flawed because just because something has been done for a long time doesn't make it the best or only way to do it. Traditions can be valuable, but it's important to examine them critically rather than following them without question. Change or new ideas aren't necessarily wrong just because they're different.

Why Do Humans Use *Appeal to Tradition*?

Humans often feel comforted by tradition; it provides stability and a sense of continuity. Change can feel uncertain or even threatening, so people sometimes cling to traditions to avoid the discomfort of something new. However, this can limit progress and ignore better solutions that come from innovation.

How to Avoid *Appeal to Tradition*

1. Ask If Tradition Serves a Purpose

Check if the tradition has a clear benefit or if it's just a habit. Useful traditions often serve a real purpose.

2. Consider Alternatives

When you're tempted to choose tradition, think about whether there might be a better or more efficient way.

3. Question Without Disregard

Respect tradition but be open to new ideas. Asking, "Is this still the best way?" allows for both continuity and improvement.

Practice Example

Imagine someone argues, "We've always used this system at work, so we shouldn't change it." Instead of accepting this, consider asking, "Is this system still working effectively, or could a new approach improve it?"

Defending Against *Appeal to Tradition*

When someone uses this fallacy, here's how to open up the conversation for new ideas:

- **Gently Question the Purpose**

  Ask, "Does this tradition still serve a useful purpose?" This helps them reflect on the value of the tradition itself.

- **Suggest Examining Both Options**

  Say, "Could we consider the pros and cons of each approach?" This encourages a balanced view of tradition and new ideas.

- **Acknowledge Tradition, Then Suggest Evaluation**

  Try saying, "I appreciate the tradition, but let's also see if there's an even better way." This respects the tradition while staying open to improvements.

By learning to spot and question the *Appeal to Tradition* fallacy, you'll avoid getting stuck in outdated ways of thinking. Respecting the past is valuable, but so is knowing when to move forward. Speaking of moving forward, there's another mental trap that can make it hard to let go, even when it's best to do so. Let's discuss this next.

Chapter 17: The Sunk Cost Fallacy

The *Sunk Cost* fallacy happens when someone continues with a plan or idea simply because they've already invested a lot of time, money, or effort into it, even when it's no longer the best option. It's like saying, "I've spent so much time on this, I can't quit now!" This fallacy ignores whether it's still worth continuing.

Why Is *Sunk Cost* a Fallacy?

Sunk Cost is flawed because past investments shouldn't decide future actions. Rational decisions should focus on what will bring the most value going forward. Just because you've invested resources doesn't mean you should keep going if it's no longer beneficial. Letting go of what no longer serves you can be the wiser choice.

Why Do Humans Fall for the *Sunk Cost Fallacy*?

Humans often struggle with this fallacy because they don't want to feel that their time, money, or energy has been "wasted." The idea of "giving up" on something they've invested in feels like admitting defeat. However, holding onto an unwise decision can lead to even greater loss.

How to Avoid the *Sunk Cost Fallacy*

1. Focus on Future Value, Not Past Investment

Ask yourself, "Is continuing the best choice going forward?" It helps to think in terms of future benefits rather than what's already been spent.

2. Recognize When It's Time to Let Go

Accepting that past resources are "sunk" or spent can help you move on. It's okay to pivot when something no longer makes sense.

3. Think Objectively About Gains and Losses

Separate your emotional attachment from the decision. Ask, "What will bring the best results moving forward?"

Practice Example

Imagine someone says, "I've already put so much money into fixing this old car, I can't sell it now!" Instead of holding onto it for emotional reasons, a better approach might be to evaluate if selling the car and getting a reliable one would save money in the long run.

Defending Against the *Sunk Cost Fallacy*

If someone is caught in this fallacy, here's how you can help them refocus:

- **Encourage Forward-Thinking**

  Say, "Let's think about what would bring the most benefit from this point forward."

- **Point Out the Cost of Staying Stuck**

  Remind them, "Sometimes, holding on actually costs more than letting go." This can help them see the potential benefits of moving on.

- **Reframe the Decision**

Suggest, "Consider the choice as if no past investment had been made—what would you do?" This makes it easier to see the decision objectively.

By understanding the *Sunk Cost Fallacy*, you can make better choices that focus on future benefits instead of clinging to past investments. Sometimes moving forward means making wise choices about what's truly valuable — but what happens when something seems better simply because it's new?

Chapter 18: The Appeal to Novelty Fallacy

The *Appeal to Novelty* fallacy occurs when someone assumes that something is better or more valuable just because it's new. It's like saying, "This must be the best phone because it's the latest model!" While new ideas and products can bring improvements, being new doesn't automatically make something better.

Why Is *Appeal to Novelty* a Fallacy?

The *Appeal to Novelty* is flawed because it focuses on the age or "freshness" of an idea rather than its actual quality or effectiveness. New isn't always better; sometimes, older methods or ideas work just as well or even better. Making choices based solely on novelty can lead to overlooking the value of tried-and-true options.

Why Do Humans Use *Appeal to Novelty*?

Humans are often drawn to novelty because it feels exciting and forward-thinking. There's a natural curiosity about new things, which can lead people to assume that fresh ideas or inventions are superior. However, novelty alone isn't enough to make something better; it needs real evidence of improvement.

How to Avoid *Appeal to Novelty*

1. Ask for Evidence of Improvement

Before accepting something new, ask, "What makes this better than what came before it?" Look for solid reasons instead of assuming newness equals improvement.

2. Compare the Pros and Cons

Weigh the benefits of both old and new options. Sometimes, the "tried-and-true" option is still the best choice.

3. Be Cautious of Trends

Recognize that just because something is trendy or new doesn't mean it's an improvement. Focus on function and effectiveness rather than hype.

Practice Example

Imagine someone says, "This new diet must be the best because it's so popular right now!" Instead of jumping on board, ask, "What specific benefits does this diet offer that older ones don't?" This focuses on the actual value rather than just the novelty.

Defending Against *Appeal to Novelty*

When others insist something is better just because it's new, here's how to keep the focus on actual quality:

• Ask for Concrete Benefits

Say, "I understand it's new, but what specific improvements does it offer?" This brings the conversation back to the actual value.

• **Encourage Balanced Comparison**

Suggest looking at both new and old options by saying, "Let's compare it with what we know already works."

• **Question the Hype**

If something seems to be popular mainly due to its novelty, ask, "Is this truly better, or just different?" This helps separate value from mere trendiness.

By avoiding the *Appeal to Novelty*, you'll make choices based on real benefits, not just trends. But even with a clear view of what's truly valuable, there's another trap to watch for — the idea that the "middle" option is always the best choice. Let's dive into this next fallacy!

Chapter 19: The Middle Ground Fallacy

The *Middle Ground* fallacy happens when someone assumes that the truth must lie somewhere between two opposing views, just because they're different. It's like saying, "If one person thinks the earth is flat and another thinks it's round, the truth must be halfway in between!" While compromise is often useful, it doesn't automatically mean the middle option is correct.

Why Is *Middle Ground* a Fallacy?

The *Middle Ground* fallacy is flawed because it assumes that truth is always a matter of compromise. Some issues have a clear right or wrong answer, and the truth isn't necessarily in the middle. This fallacy can lead to incorrect conclusions by assuming that every disagreement requires a middle-ground solution.

Why Do Humans Use *Middle Ground*?

Humans often believe that compromise is fair and reasonable. It feels balanced to meet halfway, so the middle ground can seem like a safe choice. However, this fallacy can create problems when one side is actually correct, and meeting in the middle compromises the truth.

How to Avoid the *Middle Ground* Fallacy

1. Consider Each Side Separately

Evaluate each perspective independently to determine if one is more valid than the other. Truth isn't always found by averaging views.

2. Think Critically About Compromise

Recognize that compromise isn't always appropriate. Sometimes, one side is correct, and the middle ground is just a false solution.

3. Look for Evidence

Focus on evidence, not just balance. The side with stronger facts or reasoning might be the true answer.

Practice Example

Imagine someone says, "One person thinks climate change is real, and another doesn't, so maybe it's only partly true." Instead of accepting this middle position, look for the scientific evidence, which overwhelmingly supports climate change.

Defending Against *Middle Ground* Fallacy

When someone defaults to a middle position, here's how you can help them see the potential flaws in this approach:

- #### Ask Why They Assume Compromise Is Needed

  Say, "Is there a reason to believe the truth is in the middle, or could one side be right?" This challenges the assumption that balance is best.

• Point to the Evidence

Emphasize facts by saying, "Let's see which side the evidence supports, rather than assuming they're equally valid."

• Acknowledge Fairness, Then Redirect to Facts

Gently say, "Compromise can be fair, but it doesn't always lead to the truth. Let's focus on what's actually accurate."

By recognizing and avoiding the *Middle Ground* fallacy, you'll focus on truth over compromise, making decisions based on facts rather than perceived fairness. But even with this clarity, there's another pitfall to avoid — one that involves selectively choosing only the facts that fit a particular view!

Chapter 20: The Cherry Picking Fallacy

The *Cherry Picking* fallacy happens when someone selects only the evidence that supports their argument while ignoring evidence that contradicts it. It's like saying, "Eating chocolate is healthy because cocoa has antioxidants!" but conveniently forgetting to mention the sugar and fat in chocolate. *Cherry Picking* presents a biased view by focusing only on favorable facts.

Why Is *Cherry Picking* a Fallacy?

Cherry Picking is misleading because it doesn't give a full picture of the truth. Good arguments consider *all* relevant evidence, not just the parts that make their case look good. By ignoring contradictory evidence, *Cherry Picking* can create a one-sided view that isn't based on reality.

Why Do Humans Use *Cherry Picking*?

Humans might use *Cherry Picking* to make their case look stronger than it actually is. By ignoring inconvenient facts, they avoid facing challenges to their view. This is often done unconsciously, as humans naturally like to focus on evidence that supports their beliefs.

How to Avoid *Cherry Picking*

1. Consider All Available Evidence

Before reaching a conclusion, ask, "Am I looking at all the facts or just the ones that support my view?"

2. Include Counterpoints

Even if some evidence doesn't support your view, acknowledging it shows a balanced and fair approach. This builds credibility and demonstrates honesty.

3. Be Open to Evidence That Challenges You

Real progress happens when you can confront evidence that disagrees with your position. Being open-minded makes for stronger arguments.

Practice Example

Imagine someone claims, "Our city has great air quality because we have so many parks." This might ignore other factors, like high car emissions, that also affect air quality. To avoid *Cherry Picking*, they could include a complete look at all factors impacting air quality.

Defending Against *Cherry Picking*

When someone cherry-picks evidence, here's how to encourage a fairer discussion:

- **Ask for the Full Picture**

Say, "Is there other evidence we're not considering?" This invites a more balanced view.

• Point Out Missing Facts

If they're avoiding certain facts, mention them politely: "I think there are additional factors, like [missing evidence], that should be included."

• Encourage a Complete Analysis

Suggest saying, "Let's look at all the data, not just parts of it." This helps keep the discussion grounded in reality.

By learning to avoid *Cherry Picking*, you'll create stronger arguments based on a full view of the facts. But as you keep refining your reasoning, beware of another trap — one that judges ideas based on outcomes rather than truth. Ready to uncover the next fallacy?

Chapter 21: The Appeal to Consequences Fallacy

The *Appeal to Consequences* fallacy happens when someone argues that an idea must be true or false based on whether the consequences are good or bad, rather than on actual evidence. It's like saying, "Climate change can't be real because that would mean big changes in our lifestyle!" This fallacy focuses on the impact of believing something instead of whether it's true.

Why Is *Appeal to Consequences* a Fallacy?

Appeal to Consequences is flawed because truth isn't determined by how desirable or undesirable the outcome is. The truth of a claim depends on evidence, not on whether we like the results. Good arguments are based on facts and logic, not just on whether we find the consequences appealing or unpleasant.

Why Do Humans Use *Appeal to Consequences*?

Humans often use this fallacy because they're uncomfortable with the possible effects of a certain idea. Focusing on consequences instead of truth can be a form of denial or wishful thinking, allowing people to avoid facing difficult realities.

How to Avoid *Appeal to Consequences*

1. Focus on Facts, Not Feelings

Ask yourself, "Am I rejecting this idea because of how it feels, or because the evidence doesn't support it?" This keeps you grounded in facts.

2. Separate Truth from Impact

Recognize that truth and consequences are separate. Even if an outcome is undesirable, that doesn't make the idea untrue.

3. Accept Discomfort for the Sake of Accuracy

Sometimes, the truth can be uncomfortable. Accepting this helps you stay focused on accuracy rather than comfort.

Practice Example

Imagine someone says, "We can't admit that our project failed because it would hurt our reputation." Instead of focusing on the negative outcome, a better approach is to ask, "Did the project meet its goals based on the evidence?"

Defending Against *Appeal to Consequences*

When someone uses this fallacy, here's how to steer the discussion back to facts:

• Ask for Evidence First

Say, "Regardless of the outcome, what does the evidence say?" This refocuses on truth rather than impact.

- **Point Out the Difference Between Feelings and Facts**

  Gently remind them, "Our feelings about the outcome don't change the actual truth."

- **Encourage an Objective View**

  Suggest looking at the situation objectively by saying, "Let's focus on what's real, not just what's comfortable."

By recognizing the *Appeal to Consequences* fallacy, you'll base your decisions on evidence rather than wishful thinking. But sometimes, reasoning falters not because of evidence, but because something simply seems unbelievable. Let's explore this next fallacy!

Chapter 22: The Personal Incredulity Fallacy

The *Personal Incredulity* fallacy happens when someone dismisses an argument or idea because they find it difficult to understand. It's like saying, "I don't understand how evolution works, so it must be false." This fallacy treats personal difficulty in understanding as a reason to reject an idea, rather than relying on facts.

Why Is *Personal Incredulity* a Fallacy?

Personal Incredulity is flawed because the truth of an idea doesn't depend on whether someone understands it. Complexity or unfamiliarity doesn't make an idea wrong; it simply means it might require more study or explanation. Basing truth on our own understanding limits us to what we already know.

Why Do Humans Use *Personal Incredulity*?

Humans sometimes fall into this fallacy because they're more comfortable with ideas that make sense right away. When something seems too complex, the brain might default to dismissing it rather than exploring it further. But just because something is challenging doesn't mean it's incorrect.

How to Avoid *Personal Incredulity*

1. Seek to Understand Before Judging

If something seems confusing, try to learn more before rejecting it. Ask, "Is there a reason I don't understand this?"

2. Acknowledge Limits to Knowledge

Realize that not fully grasping an idea doesn't make it false. It might just mean you need more information or time to understand.

3. Be Open to Complexity

Recognize that some ideas require patience to understand. Embrace the possibility that difficult concepts might still be true.

Practice Example

Imagine someone says, "I don't get how vaccines work, so I don't trust them." Instead of dismissing vaccines, they could seek out credible sources to learn about how vaccines provide immunity, even if the science feels complex.

Defending Against *Personal Incredulity*

When someone dismisses an idea because they don't understand it, here's how you can help them see beyond their own perspective:

- #### Encourage Further Learning

    Say, "Maybe more information would help. Understanding can take time with complex ideas."

• Separate Understanding from Truth

Gently point out, "Even if it's hard to understand, that doesn't mean it's wrong." This helps them see that difficulty doesn't equal falsehood.

• Suggest Reliable Sources

If possible, recommend sources or experts that could help them learn more. Say, "Let's look for trusted information to help explain it better."

By learning to avoid the *Personal Incredulity* fallacy, you'll open yourself up to new knowledge and be more willing to explore ideas outside your comfort zone. But be cautious — just because something seems natural doesn't automatically make it better.

Chapter 23: The Appeal to Nature Fallacy

The *Appeal to Nature* fallacy happens when someone argues that something is good or right simply because it's "natural," or bad just because it's "unnatural." It's like saying, "Organic food is better just because it's natural!" While nature can offer many benefits, being natural doesn't automatically make something good, nor does being unnatural make it bad.

Why Is Appeal to Nature a Fallacy?

The *Appeal to Nature* is flawed because what's natural isn't always beneficial or safe. Poisonous plants and dangerous diseases are natural, yet they're harmful, while many life-saving medicines are "unnatural" but beneficial. Real evaluation requires looking at actual evidence.

Why Do Humans Use *Appeal to Nature*?

Humans are often drawn to the idea of nature as pure, safe, and healthy. There's an instinctive trust in things labeled as natural and a suspicion of things seen as synthetic. However, this bias can lead to overlooking the benefits of science and innovation, which often improve on nature.

How to Avoid *Appeal to Nature*

1. Evaluate Benefits, Not Labels

Look for real benefits, not just the "natural" label. Ask, "What does this actually do?"

2. Look for Evidence of Safety and Effectiveness

Something's value should be based on research and evidence, not just its source. Scientific testing often gives better insight than assumptions about naturalness.

3. Separate Feelings from Facts

Acknowledge that the "natural" label may feel safe, but that feeling isn't always backed by reality. Feelings don't determine effectiveness or safety.

Practice Example

Imagine someone claims, "Herbal remedies are always better because they're natural." Instead of assuming this, they could look for evidence comparing the effectiveness and safety of herbal remedies versus regulated medications.

Defending Against *Appeal to Nature*

When someone insists that natural things are better, here's how to gently refocus on actual evidence:

• Ask for Evidence Beyond Labels

Say, "I see it's natural, but do we know it's effective?" This shifts focus to evidence of results.

- **Point Out That Nature Can Be Harmful**

  Gently remind them, "Natural things aren't always safe—think of poison ivy!" This helps them recognize that nature isn't automatically good.

- **Encourage Evaluation Based on Effectiveness**

  Suggest saying, "Let's look at what works best, not just what's natural." This helps keep the conversation balanced and grounded in results.

By understanding and avoiding the *Appeal to Nature* fallacy, you'll make decisions based on effectiveness rather than simply on what's "natural." But as you sharpen your logical thinking, there's another trap to watch for — one that tries to protect a claim by redefining it.

Chapter 24: The No True Scotsman Fallacy

The *No True Scotsman* fallacy happens when someone redefines a group to exclude individuals or counterexamples that don't fit their argument. It's like saying, "No real artist would use digital tools." When someone points out a famous artist who does, they respond, "Well, no *true* artist would."

Why Is *No True Scotsman* a Fallacy?

No True Scotsman is flawed because it uses an arbitrary redefinition to defend a point. Instead of addressing counterexamples or valid exceptions, it changes the group's definition to avoid them. Real arguments should deal with exceptions directly, not redefine terms to fit a narrative.

Why Do Humans Use *No True Scotsman*?

Humans sometimes use this fallacy because they want to protect a belief from criticism. When something challenges an identity or group they feel attached to, they may try to "purify" the group by excluding members or ideas that don't align.

How to Avoid *No True Scotsman*

1. Recognize Exceptions and Differences

Acknowledge that diversity exists within groups. Just because some members act differently doesn't mean they don't belong.

2. Be Open to Challenging Examples

Accept counterexamples as part of the discussion rather than excluding them. This helps strengthen understanding rather than limit it.

3. Avoid Defining Identity Narrowly

When defending a group or identity, use broader definitions that include valid diversity within the group.

Practice Example

Imagine someone says, "No true gamer would play on easy mode." When a gamer who does play on easy mode is mentioned, they respond, "Well, they're not a true gamer." Instead of redefining the group, a more open perspective accepts that gamers play at all levels.

Defending Against *No True Scotsman*

When someone uses this fallacy, here's how to encourage a more inclusive view:

- **Ask Why They're Excluding**

Say, "Why can't this person belong just because they're different?" This gently challenges their redefinition.

• Point Out Diversity in the Group

Suggest, "Groups can be diverse—people don't have to fit a narrow definition to belong."

• Encourage Broader Thinking

Remind them, "Let's recognize that there's room for different views within this group." This helps avoid narrow labels.

By recognizing the *No True Scotsman* fallacy, you'll promote broader thinking and allow for diversity within groups. Each fallacy you learn makes your arguments clearer. But be careful — even the facts themselves can be misleading if only certain ones are chosen to fit a pattern!

Chapter 25: The Texas Sharpshooter Fallacy

The *Texas Sharpshooter* fallacy happens when someone focuses only on data that supports their argument, ignoring data that doesn't fit. It's like shooting at the side of a barn, then drawing a target around the bullet holes and saying, "Look how accurate I am!"

Why Is *Texas Sharpshooter* a Fallacy?

The *Texas Sharpshooter* fallacy is misleading because it makes connections between random patterns, rather than looking at the full picture. By selectively choosing data points, it can create an illusion of accuracy or causation that isn't truly there. Real analysis considers *all* the evidence, not just the convenient parts.

Why Do Humans Use *Texas Sharpshooter*?

Humans tend to notice patterns and may even create them unintentionally. It can feel satisfying to make data "fit" a certain narrative, especially when it supports an idea or goal. By focusing only on specific details, people may overlook the full context or counterevidence that tells a different story.

How to Avoid *Texas Sharpshooter*

1. Look at All the Data, Not Just What Fits

Ask, "Am I ignoring any facts that don't fit my idea?" A complete view includes all evidence, even inconvenient facts.

2. Avoid Making Patterns from Coincidence

Be cautious about connecting data points randomly. Correlation doesn't equal causation, and sometimes patterns are just coincidence.

3. Be Willing to Adjust Your Conclusions

If the full data doesn't support your view, be open to changing your conclusion. True understanding comes from accuracy, not convenience.

Practice Example

Imagine someone says, "Most top students drink coffee, so coffee must make people smarter." Instead of just looking at coffee-drinking students, a more accurate analysis would look at all students, coffee-drinkers and non-coffee-drinkers, to see if coffee actually has an impact.

Defending Against *Texas Sharpshooter*

If someone is using this fallacy, here's how to encourage them to look at the full picture:

- **Ask About Missing Data**

    Say, "Are there any data points we're not considering?" This encourages a broader view.

- **Point Out the Full Range of Evidence**

  Politely remind them, "To be fair, we should look at all the evidence, not just parts that match." This keeps the conversation balanced.

- **Encourage a Complete Analysis**

  Suggest saying, "Let's see if the whole set of data supports this idea." This keeps the focus on accuracy rather than selective points.

By avoiding the *Texas Sharpshooter* fallacy, you'll be able to make well-rounded arguments based on full evidence, not selective patterns. But sometimes, even with a lot of data, it's easy to overlook the stories that don't make it through. Let's unpack this next fallacy!

Chapter 26: The Survivorship Bias Fallacy

The *Survivorship Bias* fallacy occurs when someone focuses only on successful examples while ignoring failures, leading to a skewed understanding of reality. It's like saying, "Look at all the successful entrepreneurs who dropped out of college — you don't need a degree to succeed!" without considering the many dropouts who didn't become successful. This fallacy creates an overly optimistic or one-sided view by ignoring the full range of outcomes.

Why Is *Survivorship Bias* a Fallacy?

Survivorship Bias is misleading because it only looks at the "survivors" or successful examples, ignoring the "non-survivors" who didn't achieve the same results. This limited view can give people the wrong impression of what's likely or effective, leading to unrealistic expectations. For balanced conclusions, it's important to consider all data, not just the positive cases.

Why Do Humans Use *Survivorship Bias*?

Humans often focus on success stories because they're inspiring and give us hope. Hearing about successful people or outcomes can make us feel motivated, but it can also lead to a skewed view if we don't consider failures. Recognizing this bias helps us form more realistic expectations based on the complete picture.

How to *Avoid Survivorship* Bias

1. Look for "Invisible" Data

Ask yourself, "Am I only seeing the successful cases?" Check if there's information missing about those who didn't succeed.

2. Consider the Full Range of Outcomes

Try to understand both successes and failures. Ask, "What happened to people who tried and didn't make it?"

3. Be Realistic About Likelihood

Understand that not everyone reaches the same results. Focusing on both success and failure helps set realistic expectations.

Practice Example

Imagine someone says, "Successful authors write every day, so that's the key to success." To avoid *Survivorship Bias*, consider asking, "What about authors who wrote every day but didn't succeed?" This provides a more realistic view of success.

Defending Against *Survivorship Bias*

When someone falls into *Survivorship Bias*, here's how to bring balance to the conversation:

• Ask About the Less Visible Data

Say, "Are we also considering people who didn't succeed?" This invites a broader view.

• Remind Them of All Outcomes

Suggest saying, "Success stories are inspiring, but failures provide important lessons too."

• Encourage Balanced Examples

Suggest looking for both success and failure stories by saying, "Let's see the complete picture for a more realistic view."

By understanding *Survivorship Bias*, you'll avoid forming conclusions based only on visible successes. But even when the evidence is clear, some arguments shift the standards to stay one step ahead. Ready to tackle this next fallacy?

Chapter 27: The Moving the Goalposts Fallacy

The *Moving the Goalposts* fallacy occurs when someone keeps changing the criteria for "proof" to avoid accepting an argument. It's like saying, "If you show me one study that supports this, I'll believe it," and then, after seeing the study, saying, "Well, I need three studies, actually!"

Why Is *Moving the Goalposts* a Fallacy?

Moving the Goalposts is flawed because it prevents genuine progress in a discussion. By continuously raising the standards for "acceptable proof," it creates a situation where no amount of evidence will satisfy. Honest discussions should have clear, consistent criteria for what counts as proof, rather than constantly changing expectations.

Why Do Humans Use *Moving the Goalposts*?

Humans often use this fallacy when they're resistant to changing their beliefs. By changing the requirements for evidence, they avoid facing evidence that challenges their viewpoint. It's a way to keep from being "convinced" by shifting what's needed to persuade them.

How to Avoid *Moving the Goalposts*

1. Set Clear Standards for Proof

Decide in advance what will count as sufficient evidence. Ask yourself, "What level of proof would satisfy me?"

2. Be Willing to Accept Valid Evidence

Don't keep raising the bar if evidence meets the original standards. Avoid creating new requirements just to avoid admitting you're wrong.

3. Stay Consistent in Arguments

Don't change the standards mid-discussion. Consistency helps keep arguments honest and fair.

Practice Example

Imagine someone says, "If you can find one article proving this, I'll believe it." When shown an article, they respond, "Actually, I need multiple studies from major journals." Instead of genuinely considering the evidence, they keep shifting the requirements.

Defending Against *Moving the Goalposts*

If someone is moving the goalposts, here's how to encourage a fair discussion:

• Ask for Clear Standards

Say, "Can we agree on what counts as enough evidence?" This sets a standard from the start.

• Hold Them to Original Criteria

If they try to change the goal, politely remind them, "You said this would be enough evidence. Let's stick with that."

• Encourage Consistency in Expectations

Gently suggest saying, "Changing the standards makes it hard to find common ground. Can we agree to be consistent?"

By recognizing the *Moving the Goalposts* fallacy, you'll keep discussions fair and grounded in clear standards. But sometimes, rather than changing the standards, arguments shift focus by amplifying fear instead. Let's explore this next fallacy!

Chapter 28: The Scare Tactic Fallacy

The *Scare Tactic* Fallacy happens when someone tries to persuade others by fear rather than presenting logical reasons. It's like saying, "If we don't ban this technology, it will take over our lives!" Here, the argument relies on fear to make people agree rather than offering a well-reasoned point.

Why Is the *Scare Tactic* Fallacy a Fallacy?

The *Scare Tactic* Fallacy is flawed because emotions like fear don't prove whether something is actually dangerous or problematic. Rational thinking requires examining evidence rather than being swayed by fear, which can lead to rushed or exaggerated decisions. Sound reasoning focuses on facts, not the heightened emotions that fear brings.

Why Do Humans Use the *Scare Tactic* Fallacy?

Humans often fall into this fallacy because fear can be a powerful motivator. It's easier to evoke an emotional response than to construct a logical argument, especially when the goal is to influence someone's decisions quickly. Recognizing this tendency helps us remain calm and evaluate the actual risks of a situation, rather than being pulled along by fear.

How to Avoid the *Scare Tactic* Fallacy

1. Evaluate the Evidence Behind the Threat

Ask yourself, "Is there solid evidence that this situation is truly dangerous?"

2. Separate Emotion from Facts

Consider whether the argument is based on fear alone or backed by data.

3. Seek a Balanced Perspective

Avoid letting worst-case scenarios guide your decisions without considering other possibilities.

Practice Example

Imagine someone says, "If we don't enforce this curfew, crime will spiral out of control!" This is an example of the *Scare Tactic* Fallacy because it uses fear to influence decisions rather than presenting data on crime or examining whether a curfew is effective. A more logical approach would include statistics and other facts to support the need for a curfew.

Defending Against the *Scare Tactic* Fallacy

When someone tries to persuade you using fear, here's how to bring the discussion back to logic:

• Ask for Evidence

Say, "Is there any data that supports this as a serious risk?"

- **Encourage Thinking About Facts Over Emotions**

Suggest, "Let's focus on the facts rather than on how scary it sounds."

- **Remind Them That Fear Doesn't Equal Risk**

Gently add, "Fear alone doesn't prove something is dangerous—it just feels that way."

By recognizing the *Scare Tactic* Fallacy, you'll stay calm and focused on evidence, making decisions based on facts rather than fear. But fear isn't the only force that can sway an argument — sometimes, it's personal stories that lead us off track. Let's review this next fallacy!

Chapter 29: The Appeal to Personal Experience Fallacy

The *Appeal to Personal Experience* fallacy happens when someone argues their personal experience proves a general truth, instead of broad reliable evidence. It's like saying, "I've never gotten sick from not washing my hands, so handwashing isn't necessary."

Why Is *Appeal to Personal Experience* a Fallacy?

The *Appeal to Personal Experience* is flawed because one person's experience doesn't represent the whole picture. True claims, especially those about health, science, or general rules, need consistent evidence from many cases, not just one.

Why Do Humans Use *Appeal to Personal Experience*?

Humans often trust their own experiences because they're direct and memorable. It's natural to believe what we see or feel firsthand, but personal experience doesn't always capture the full reality. Recognizing this can help us seek broader, more reliable evidence.

How to Avoid Appeal to *Personal Experience*

1. Look for Larger Patterns

Ask yourself, "Does this apply to just me, or to most people?" Broad trends are more reliable than personal examples.

2. Acknowledge Individual Differences

Recognize that everyone's experience is unique and doesn't always represent general truth.

3. Rely on Research

Use studies, surveys, or expert consensus when making claims about broad truths. These sources represent more people and are less likely to be skewed by individual differences.

Practice Example

Imagine someone says, "I never exercise, and I'm perfectly healthy, so exercise isn't that important." While this might be true for them, most evidence shows exercise benefits health. Relying on a single experience misses the larger, proven trend.

Defending Against *Appeal to Personal Experience*

When someone relies on personal experience to make a general claim, here's how to steer the discussion toward broader evidence:

- **Ask About Larger Evidence**

Say, "That's interesting, but what does the broader evidence say?" This shifts focus from individual to general data.

- **Acknowledge Their Experience, Then Broaden the View**

  Gently respond, "I understand that worked for you, but let's consider what studies show for most people."

- **Encourage Objectivity**

  Remind them, "Personal experiences can vary a lot, so it's good to rely on larger studies." This emphasizes the need for reliable, comprehensive data.

By understanding the *Appeal to Personal Experience* fallacy, you'll be able to recognize when individual cases don't necessarily represent general truths. But be careful — sometimes, the opposite mistake happens, where it's assumed that what's true for each part must be true for the whole!

Good Pieces   The Whole

Chapter 30: The Composition Fallacy

The *Composition fallacy* occurs when someone assumes that what's true of individual parts must also be true of the whole. It's like saying, "Each player on the team is a star, so the team must be unbeatable!" While each part may be impressive on its own, they don't automatically reflect the complete picture.

Why Is *Composition* a Fallacy?

The *Composition fallacy* is flawed because individual parts don't always add up in the way we might expect. Each part might work well alone, but when combined, they don't necessarily produce the same results. Good reasoning requires looking at the whole and understanding how the parts work together, rather than assuming qualities of the parts directly transfer to the whole.

Why Do Humans Use Composition?

Humans naturally assume that impressive parts will create an impressive whole. This fallacy often occurs when we focus on individual strengths or qualities without considering how parts interact in combination. Recognizing this tendency can help us evaluate wholes more accurately.

How to Avoid Composition

1. Examine How Parts Work Together

Consider whether the parts actually combine in a way that makes the whole better. Ask, "Do these parts interact effectively?"

2. Avoid Generalizing from Individuals to Groups

Just because something is true of one member or part doesn't mean it's true of the entire group.

3. Look for Evidence of Group Performance

Instead of assuming a strong team based on strong players, look at how they perform together. The whole might have different dynamics.

Practice Example

Imagine someone says, "All the ingredients in this dish are delicious, so the dish must be delicious too." However, even tasty ingredients can create an unpleasant combination if they don't work well together. To avoid this fallacy, consider how the ingredients interact as a whole.

Defending Against *Composition*

When someone assumes that the qualities of individual parts apply to the whole, here's how to respond:

- ### Ask About Interaction

    Say, "How do the parts actually work together?" This encourages them to think about how parts interact within the whole.

- **Point Out Differences Between Parts and Wholes**

Politely remind them, "Sometimes a group has different qualities than its members."

- **Suggest Looking at Group Evidence**

Encourage them by saying, "Let's see if there's evidence about the whole, not just the parts." This keeps the focus on group performance or combination effects.

By avoiding the *Composition* fallacy, you'll make better evaluations about groups, teams, and combinations, focusing on how parts actually work together. But there's an opposite trap to watch out for — the assumption that what's true for the whole must be true for each part.

Chapter 31: The Division Fallacy

The *Division* fallacy is the opposite of the *Composition* fallacy. It happens when someone assumes that what's true of the whole must also be true of each individual part. It's like saying, "This cake is delicious, so every ingredient must be delicious too!"

Why Is *Division* a Fallacy?

The *Division* fallacy is flawed because qualities of the whole don't always transfer to its parts. A whole can have a certain characteristic that doesn't appear in each of its parts individually. Clear thinking requires understanding that parts can differ from the whole they're part of.

Why Do Humans Use *Division*?

Humans often assume that parts will have the same qualities as the whole because it feels consistent and logical. However, this assumption overlooks the complexity of how parts can interact differently within the whole. Understanding this fallacy helps us see that parts and wholes aren't always the same.

How to Avoid *Division*

1. Consider Parts Separately

Ask yourself, "Do the qualities of the whole really apply to each part?" Think about the unique qualities of each component.

2. Avoid Generalizing from Whole to Parts

Recognize that parts don't always share the same characteristics as a whole.

3. Examine Each Part on Its Own

When evaluating parts, consider them individually rather than assuming they inherit the whole's qualities.

Practice Example

Imagine someone says, "This company is highly successful, so every department must be great too." However, even a successful company can have weaker areas or departments that don't perform as well as the company as a whole. To avoid the Division fallacy, evaluate each part on its own.

Defending Against *Division*

When someone makes an assumption that each part shares the qualities of the whole, here's how to encourage clearer thinking:

- **Point Out the Difference Between Parts and Wholes**

Say, "Just because the whole is successful doesn't mean each part has to be." This helps clarify that qualities don't always transfer.

- **Encourage Evaluating Each Part Separately**

  Suggest saying, "Let's look at each part individually to see how they really perform."

- **Remind Them That Parts Can Differ from the Whole**

  Politely add, "Sometimes, parts are very different from the larger whole." This opens up the possibility for a more nuanced view.

By understanding the *Division* fallacy, you'll recognize that just because a whole has certain qualities doesn't mean each part does. Great job — each fallacy you master adds to your logical toolkit! Now, let's look at a fallacy that shifts focus from the argument itself to assumptions about why someone believes it.

Chapter 32: The Bulverism Fallacy

The *Bulverism* Fallacy happens when someone dismisses an argument not by addressing its content, but by assuming it must be wrong due to the person's supposed reasons or motives for believing it. It's like saying, "You only support that idea because you're young and idealistic," rather than addressing the argument itself. Here, the argument is rejected by focusing on a presumed bias or background rather than its actual reasoning.

Why Is *Bulverism* a Fallacy?

Bulverism is flawed because it assumes that if a person has a certain reason for their belief, the belief itself must be wrong. But an argument's validity doesn't depend on the person making it — it depends on facts, evidence, and reasoning. Rational thinking requires evaluating ideas on their own merits, not making assumptions based on who holds them.

Why Do Humans Use *Bulverism*?

Humans often fall into this fallacy because it's easier to question a person's motives than to engage with their arguments. We're naturally inclined to assume others are biased, especially if we disagree with them, but this can lead to unfair dismissals and missed opportunities for genuine understanding. Recognizing this tendency helps us focus on the actual argument rather than on assumptions about the person making it.

How to Avoid *Bulverism*

1. Separate the Argument from the Person

Ask yourself, "Am I rejecting this idea because of the argument itself, or because of who is saying it?"

2. Engage with the Argument's Logic

Focus on whether the argument is backed by sound reasoning and evidence.

3. Avoid Assuming a Person's Bias as Proof

Remember, even if someone has a personal reason for their view, the argument itself could still be valid.

Practice Example

Imagine someone says, "Climate change is a serious issue we need to address," and the response is, "You're only saying that because you're young and idealistic." This is an example of *Bulverism*, as it dismisses the argument by assuming a reason for it rather than addressing the actual issue. A more rational approach would evaluate the evidence for climate change independently of the speaker's age or personality.

Defending Against the *Bulverism* Fallacy

When someone dismisses an argument based on presumed motives, here's how to steer the conversation back to the actual points:

- **Ask for Evidence-Based Discussion**

Say, "Could we focus on the evidence or reasoning behind this point?"

- **Encourage Evaluating the Argument Itself**

Suggest, "Let's consider the idea on its own, apart from personal reasons."

- **Point Out That Motives Don't Determine Validity**

Gently add, "Even if someone has a personal reason for their belief, the argument still deserves to be addressed on its own terms."

By recognizing the *Bulverism* Fallacy, you'll be able to engage with ideas fairly, addressing arguments based on their content rather than assuming motives. But even with fair-minded reasoning, it's easy to fall into another trap — dismissing ideas just because they're not perfect.

Chapter 33: The Nirvana Fallacy

The *Nirvana* fallacy happens when someone dismisses a realistic solution because it isn't "perfect." It's like saying, "Recycling isn't worth doing because it doesn't eliminate all waste." This fallacy ignores the value of practical solutions simply because they have some flaws or don't achieve perfection.

Why Is *Nirvana* a Fallacy?

The *Nirvana* fallacy is flawed because it holds practical solutions to an impossible standard. While most solutions have limitations, they still bring positive change. Rejecting realistic options because they aren't flawless can prevent progress.

Why Do Humans Use *Nirvana* Fallacy?

Humans often fall into this fallacy when they want an ideal solution. It can feel satisfying to imagine perfection, but this mindset can prevent people from taking steps that could still make a difference. By learning to accept workable solutions, we avoid rejecting useful options in search of unattainable ones.

How to Avoid *Nirvana* Fallacy

1. Focus on Realistic Improvements

Recognize that partial solutions can still have value. Ask, "Does this solution make things better, even if it's not perfect?"

2. Acknowledge Trade-offs

Most solutions involve trade-offs. Accepting this can help you appreciate solutions that work well enough, even with limitations.

3. Avoid "All-or-Nothing" Thinking

Remember that small changes can add up. It doesn't have to be perfect to be valuable.

Practice Example

Imagine someone says, "Public transportation isn't worth improving because it doesn't eliminate all traffic." Instead of focusing on perfection, consider the realistic improvements that better public transportation can make in reducing traffic and pollution, even if it's not a complete solution.

Defending Against *Nirvana* Fallacy

When someone insists on rejecting realistic solutions, here's how to refocus on practical benefits:

- **Emphasize the Value of Partial Solutions**

Say, "Even if it's not perfect, it still brings benefits." This helps them see the value in incremental change.

- **Point Out That Perfection Is Rarely Possible**

Gently remind them, "Most solutions have limits, but that doesn't mean they're useless."

• Encourage Taking Steps Forward

Suggest saying, "Let's work with what we can achieve now." This keeps the conversation focused on positive, practical action.

By recognizing the *Nirvana* fallacy, you'll embrace practical solutions and avoid getting stuck in the search for perfection. Excellent work—each fallacy you understand brings you closer to balanced, effective thinking. But there's another trap to watch for — assuming that what "should" be true automatically "is" true.

Chapter 34: The Moralistic Fallacy

The *Moralistic* Fallacy happens when someone assumes that what *ought* to be true according to morals or ideals *must* be true in reality. It's like saying, "Violence shouldn't exist, so humans are naturally peaceful." This fallacy mistakes ideal or moral beliefs for actual facts about the world.

Why Is the *Moralistic* Fallacy a Fallacy?

The *Moralistic* Fallacy is flawed because reality doesn't always match our ideals. Good reasoning requires looking at facts as they are, not as we wish them to be. If we ignore reality for ideals, we miss understanding the world accurately.

Why Do Humans Use the *Moralistic* Fallacy?

Humans often fall into the Moralistic Fallacy because they want the world to align with their values and ideals. It's comforting to believe that what is morally "good" is also true. But learning to see the world as it is, rather than as we wish it to be, leads to clearer thinking and more effective solutions.

How to Avoid the *Moralistic* Fallacy

1. Separate Morals from Facts

Recognize that something being ideal doesn't make it true. Ask yourself, "Am I letting my ideals affect my view of reality?"

2. Consider Realistic Evidence

Evaluate claims based on actual evidence, not just what seems morally right.

3. Accept Reality, Even if Imperfect

Acknowledge that reality often includes things we don't like. Accepting this helps us address problems more effectively.

Practice Example

Imagine someone says, "Humans are naturally good because violence and dishonesty are morally wrong." While peace and honesty are ideals, history shows that human behavior can include aggression and deceit. Recognizing this doesn't mean accepting wrongdoing — it simply acknowledges reality as it is.

Defending Against the *Moralistic* Fallacy

When someone assumes reality should align with ideals, here's how to keep the focus on facts:

• Separate Morals from Evidence

Say, "Just because we believe something should be true doesn't make it a fact."

• Point Out that Reality May Differ

Gently remind them, "Reality isn't always ideal, but we can work with what's real to make things better."

- **Encourage Facing Facts to Create Change**
  Suggest saying, "Understanding reality helps us know what we need to work on." This shifts the focus to constructive actions based on facts.

By recognizing the *Moralistic* Fallacy, you'll be able to view the world clearly and work toward change based on real evidence. Great job! But watch out — sometimes, people deflect criticism by pointing fingers back at others. Let's dig into this next fallacy!

Chapter 35: The Appeal to Hypocrisy (Tu Quoque) Fallacy

The *Appeal to Hypocrisy* fallacy, also known as *Tu Quoque* (Latin for "You too"), occurs when someone responds to criticism by accusing the critic of the same flaw. It's like saying, "You can't tell me to save money because you spend too much yourself!" This fallacy dodges the issue by shifting focus to the critic's behavior instead of addressing the argument.

Why Is *Appeal to Hypocrisy* a Fallacy?

The *Appeal to Hypocrisy* is flawed because pointing out hypocrisy doesn't invalidate an argument. A claim can be true regardless of the speaker's behavior. Good reasoning focuses on the content of the argument.

Why Do Humans Use *Appeal to Hypocrisy*?

Humans often use this fallacy because it's easier to deflect criticism than to address it. By focusing on the other person's actions, they avoid facing the criticism. Recognizing this tendency helps us focus on the issue rather than shifting blame.

How to Avoid *Appeal to Hypocrisy*

1. Focus on the Argument, Not the Person

Separate the argument from who's making it. Ask yourself, "Is the claim true, regardless of who's saying it?"

2. Acknowledge Fair Criticism

If someone makes a valid point, address it instead of deflecting. This helps keep the conversation constructive.

3. Remember that Behavior Doesn't Change Facts

A fact remains a fact, even if the person stating it is inconsistent.

Practice Example

Imagine someone says, "We should recycle more to reduce waste," and the response is, "Why should I listen to you? You never recycle!" Instead of focusing on the person's actions, consider the value of recycling itself.

Defending Against *Appeal to Hypocrisy*

When someone tries to dodge an argument by pointing out hypocrisy, here's how to bring focus back to the main point:

• Remind Them to Focus on the Issue

Say, "Let's focus on the argument itself rather than each other's actions."

- **Acknowledge Their Point, Then Refocus**

  If they bring up your flaws, respond with, "I understand, but let's stick to the main point."

- **Point Out That Behavior Doesn't Change Facts**

  Remind them, "Whether I do it or not doesn't affect whether it's a good idea."

By recognizing the *Appeal to Hypocrisy* fallacy, you'll keep discussions on topic and focus on ideas rather than deflections. But there's another trap to watch out for — one that relies on sympathy instead of solid reasoning. Let's discuss this next fallacy!

Chapter 36: The Appeal to Pity Fallacy

The *Appeal to Pity* fallacy occurs when someone tries to win an argument by making you feel sorry for them, instead of providing logical reasons. It's like saying, "You should give me an A on my test because I studied so hard and didn't get any sleep!" Here, the person is relying on sympathy, not on actual evidence.

Why Is *Appeal to Pity* a Fallacy?

The *Appeal to Pity* is flawed because emotional appeals don't change the facts. Good arguments are based on evidence and reason, not emotions. While sympathy and understanding are valuable, they don't replace the need for logical reasons in decision-making or arguments.

Why Do Humans Use *Appeal to Pity*?

Humans use the Appeal to Pity when they feel vulnerable or want empathy. It's natural to seek understanding, especially when we're going through something difficult. But while pity can be important in friendships, it doesn't make a strong argument for a particular action or belief.

How to Avoid *Appeal to Pity*

1. Focus on Evidence Over Emotions

When making an argument, ask yourself, "Am I providing facts, or am I relying on emotions?"

2. Acknowledge Emotions Separately

Recognize emotions without letting them drive the argument. Consider saying, "I understand this is tough, but let's look at the facts."

3. Look for Real Support for Claims

Make sure your reasoning is grounded in evidence, not just emotional appeals.

Practice Example

Imagine someone says, "I really deserve the promotion because I've been struggling lately and need the extra income." While this may be true, promotions are typically based on job performance, not personal circumstances.

Defending Against *Appeal to Pity*

When someone tries to use an *Appeal to Pity*, here's how to respond empathetically but logically:

• Acknowledge Their Feelings

Say, "I understand how you feel, but we need to focus on the main issue."

• Bring the Discussion Back to Facts

Gently add, "Let's look at the facts behind the argument." This keeps the conversation grounded.

- **Suggest Separating Emotion and Reason**

  Mention, "Emotions are valid, but for this decision, we need objective reasons." This approach shows understanding without letting emotions guide the outcome.

By recognizing the *Appeal to Pity*, you'll make decisions based on reason rather than emotion alone. But even with logic on your side, it's easy to overlook relevant information — especially when probabilities and averages come into play. Let's explore this topic further!

Chapter 37: The Base Rate Fallacy

The *Base Rate* fallacy happens when someone ignores general statistical information (the "base rate") in favor of specific information, usually about an unusual event. It's like saying, "I know smoking isn't good for health, but my grandfather smoked every day and lived to be 95!" Here, the base rate — the health risks of smoking for most people — is ignored in favor of a single unusual case.

Why Is *Base Rate* Fallacy a Fallacy?

The *Base Rate* fallacy is flawed because it ignores the broader context and focuses on exceptions rather than the rule. Just because an unusual outcome happened doesn't mean it's likely. General trends and statistics provide a more reliable basis for conclusions than isolated stories.

Why Do Humans Use the *Base Rate* Fallacy?

Humans often fall into this fallacy because personal stories are vivid and memorable. It's natural to give more weight to specific, dramatic cases than to general data, but recognizing this helps us rely on statistics for a clearer understanding of likelihoods.

How to Avoid Base Rate Fallacy

1. Focus on the Bigger Picture

Ask yourself, "What do the general statistics say, beyond just a few individual cases?"

2. Consider Probability, Not Just Possibility

Remember that unusual cases are possible but not typical. Rely on base rates for reliable information.

3. Separate Stories from Statistics

Personal stories are meaningful but can be misleading. For decisions, consider broader data.

Practice Example

Imagine someone says, "My friend won the lottery, so I should buy tickets too!" The base rate, or the actual odds of winning, suggests the chances of winning are extremely low, even if one person won.

Defending Against *Base Rate* Fallacy

When someone ignores base rates, here's how to help them consider the full picture:

• Ask About the General Data

Say, "What do most cases show?" This shifts the focus back to typical outcomes.

• Encourage Looking at Likelihood

Gently add, "Even if it happened once, that doesn't make it common."

- **Highlight Probability Over Possibility**

  Suggest saying, "Just because something's possible doesn't make it probable." This helps ground the discussion in realistic outcomes.

By recognizing the Base Rate fallacy, you'll avoid being misled by rare events and make decisions based on the most likely outcomes. However, there's another trap to watch for — one that judges ideas solely based on their origins, rather than their actual merit.

Chapter 38: The Genetic Fallacy

The *Genetic Fallacy* occurs when someone dismisses or supports an argument based on its origin rather than on its actual merit. It's like saying, "This idea came from a famous scientist, so it must be true," or "That proposal was suggested by someone inexperienced, so it must be wrong." Here, the focus is not on the idea's actual content or value.

Why Is This a Fallacy?

The *Genetic* Fallacy is flawed because where an idea comes from doesn't determine its truth. Good ideas can come from surprising or unlikely sources, while even experts can have incorrect ideas. Sound reasoning means evaluating the content of a claim on its own terms, not on the background or identity of its origin.

Why Do Humans Use the *Genetic* Fallacy?

Humans sometimes rely on the *Genetic* Fallacy to avoid engaging with ideas they find difficult or uncomfortable. It can feel easier to accept or reject an argument based on the source alone rather than evaluating its actual merits. Recognizing this fallacy helps us consider ideas more fairly.

How to Avoid the *Genetic* Fallacy

1. Evaluate Content Over Source

Ask, "Is this argument valid based on its own merits, not just on who said it?"

2. Separate Idea from Origin

Recognize that even unlikely or disliked sources can offer useful insights.

3. Focus on Evidence

Base your conclusions on facts or reasoning, not on the history of where the idea came from.

Practice Example

Imagine someone says, "That study must be wrong because it was funded by a controversial organization." While funding can create potential biases, it doesn't automatically invalidate the study. A better approach would be to examine the study's methods and evidence.

Defending Against the *Genetic* Fallacy

When someone dismisses an idea based on its origin, here's how to encourage them to consider the content:

- **Shift Focus to the Argument**

  Say, "Let's look at the argument itself rather than focusing on where it came from."

- **Encourage Judging Based on Merit**

  Suggest, "Sometimes good ideas come from unexpected places. Let's see if it stands on its own."

• Point Out that Origins Don't Change Facts

Gently remind them, "The truth of an idea doesn't depend on who came up with it."

By understanding the *Genetic* Fallacy, you'll focus on ideas rather than relying on the source alone. But remember: Sometimes, an argument rests on what isn't said rather than what is. Let's discuss this next fallacy!

Chapter 39: The Argument from Silence Fallacy

The *Argument from* Silence fallacy happens when someone concludes that something is true or false based solely on a lack of evidence or silence. It's like saying, "There's no mention of dragons in historical records, so they must have existed!"

Why Is *Argument from Silence* a Fallacy?

The *Argument from Silence* is flawed because silence or a lack of information doesn't mean something did or didn't happen. There could be many reasons for missing evidence, such as incomplete records or information that wasn't preserved. Sound arguments require positive evidence, not just the absence of it.

Why Do Humans Use *Argument from Silence*?

Humans use this fallacy when they feel confident in drawing conclusions from incomplete information. When there's no direct evidence to prove or disprove something, it can be tempting to assume silence supports one's preferred view. Recognizing this fallacy helps us remember that evidence is required to make solid claims.

How to Avoid *Argument from Silence*

1. Avoid Drawing Conclusions from Lack of Evidence

Remind yourself, "Just because there's no evidence doesn't mean something is true or false."

2. Look for Positive Evidence

Ask, "Is there any direct evidence to support this claim?" This ensures you're basing beliefs on information rather than absence.

3. Recognize Gaps as Inconclusive

Silence or missing records can mean many things. Avoid assigning meaning to what isn't there.

Practice Example

Imagine someone says, "There's no record of anyone questioning the king, so everyone must have agreed with him." Just because there's no record doesn't mean there was unanimous support; it might mean dissent wasn't recorded or that records were lost.

Defending Against *Argument from Silence*

When someone uses this fallacy, here's how to encourage them to look for real evidence:

• Ask for Positive Evidence

Say, "Is there actual evidence that supports this claim, or just silence?"

- **Remind Them That Silence Is Inconclusive**

Gently mention, "Not having evidence doesn't prove anything by itself."

- **Encourage Patience Until Evidence Appears**

Suggest saying, "Let's wait until we have direct evidence before drawing a conclusion."

By understanding the *Argument from Silence* fallacy, you'll avoid making assumptions based on missing information. But watch out — some arguments claim that truth is simply a matter of perspective. Let's unpack this next fallacy!

Chapter 40: The Relativist Fallacy

The *Relativist* Fallacy occurs when someone rejects a claim as untrue simply because they believe it doesn't apply to them or their group. It's like saying, "That might be true for you, but it's not true for me," even when the topic is something objective, like a scientific fact or a well-established principle. This fallacy assumes that all truth is subjective or relative, which isn't always the case.

Why Is *Relativist* a Fallacy?

The *Relativist* Fallacy is flawed because some truths are objective — they're true regardless of personal belief. Just because someone doesn't want to accept a fact doesn't change its validity. Real understanding means distinguishing between subjective preferences (which vary) and objective truths (which don't depend on opinions).

Why Do Humans Use the Relativist Fallacy?

Humans often fall into the *Relativist* Fallacy when they want to avoid accepting a truth that challenges their worldview. It can be comforting to think, "That doesn't apply to me," but this limits growth and understanding. Recognizing this tendency helps us accept truths that apply broadly, not just personally.

How to Avoid the *Relativist* Fallacy

1. Separate Objective from Subjective

Ask, "Is this something that's true regardless of who believes it?" This helps distinguish between opinion and fact.

2. Accept That Some Facts Are Universal

Recognize that facts in areas like science, math, and history aren't personal—they apply equally to everyone.

3. Avoid Dismissing Ideas Just Because They're Uncomfortable

Be open to truths that may not fit personal preferences.

Practice Example

Imagine someone says, "Exercise is important for health," and the response is, "Maybe for most people, but not for me." Here, the person is rejecting a general health principle as if it doesn't apply to them. To avoid the *Relativist* Fallacy, they could consider evidence that shows exercise benefits everyone's health.

Defending Against the *Relativist* Fallacy

When someone uses the *Relativist* Fallacy, here's how to guide the conversation back to universal truths:

• Encourage Objective Thinking

Say, "Some things are true for everyone, even if we see them differently."

- **Ask About Evidence Supporting Universality**

  Suggest, "What evidence shows this is true for most people?" This encourages broader thinking.

- **Point Out the Difference Between Fact and Preference**

  Gently add, "Some ideas apply to everyone, even if we don't prefer them."

By understanding the *Relativist* Fallacy, you'll be able to accept objective truths and avoid dismissing facts as mere personal opinion. However, sometimes, there's a tendency to treat mere possibilities as certainties, as explained in our next fallacy.

Chapter 41: The Appeal to Probability Fallacy

The *Appeal to Probability* fallacy happens when someone assumes that because something *could* happen, it *will* happen. It's like saying, "I could win the lottery if I buy a ticket, so I'll definitely win!" While some outcomes are possible, assuming that they will happen just because they're possible is misleading.

Why Is *Appeal to Probability* a Fallacy?

The *Appeal to Probability* is flawed because it confuses possibility with certainty. Just because an outcome is possible doesn't mean it's likely. Strong reasoning requires understanding the difference between what *could* happen and what's *likely* to happen based on evidence and probability.

Why Do Humans Use the *Appeal to Probability*?

Humans often fall into this fallacy because they like to focus on exciting or preferred outcomes, even if they're unlikely. It can be tempting to believe that just because something can happen, it will happen. Recognizing this tendency helps us make more realistic assessments of risk and likelihood.

How to Avoid the *Appeal to Probability*

1. Focus on Likelihood, Not Just Possibility

Ask yourself, "What are the actual odds of this happening?" This keeps you grounded in realistic expectations.

2. Distinguish Between "Can" and "Will"

Recognize that just because something *can* happen doesn't mean it *will*.

3. Look for Statistical Evidence

Use data to understand real probabilities, not just possibilities.

Practice Example

Imagine someone says, "I could get struck by lightning while hiking, so I'm definitely going to get hit if I go outside." While it's possible, the odds of getting struck by lightning are low. A more reasonable approach would be to check weather conditions and base decisions on likely outcomes.

Defending Against the *Appeal to Probability*

When someone assumes a possibility will definitely happen, here's how to bring them back to reality:

• Ask About Likelihood

Say, "What's the actual probability of this happening?" This encourages realistic thinking.

- **Gently Point Out the Difference Between "Can" and "Will"**

  Suggest, "Just because it can happen doesn't mean it will."

- **Encourage Thinking in Terms of Realistic Risk**

  Add, "Let's look at the odds to understand how likely this really is."

By understanding the *Appeal to Probability*, you'll base your decisions on realistic odds, not just exciting possibilities. Now, there's another trap to watch for — one that dismisses issues by comparing them to larger problems. Let's explore this next fallacy!

Chapter 42: The Fallacy of Relative Privation

The *Fallacy of Relative* Privation, also known as the "Not as Bad as" fallacy, happens when someone dismisses a problem by pointing out that something else is worse. It's like saying, "Why are you upset about your broken phone? There are people who don't even have food!" While it's true that some problems are worse than others, that doesn't mean other issues aren't real or worth addressing.

Why Is *Relative Privation* a Fallacy?

The Fallacy of *Relative Privation* is flawed because it assumes that only the worst problems are worth caring about. By downplaying smaller issues, it prevents meaningful action and ignores the complexity of people's experiences. Real understanding means recognizing that multiple issues can matter, even if they're not all equally severe.

Why Do Humans Use *Relative Privation*?

Humans often fall into this fallacy to avoid addressing uncomfortable issues. By pointing out a "bigger" problem, they can deflect attention from something they don't want to deal with. Recognizing this fallacy helps us see that we can care about multiple issues without needing to rank them.

How to Avoid the Fallacy of *Relative Privation*

1. Acknowledge Multiple Levels of Importance

Recognize that just because one problem is serious, it doesn't make other issues unimportant.

2. Avoid Comparing Unrelated Issues

Stay focused on the topic at hand, rather than shifting to unrelated problems.

3. Encourage Addressing Problems Directly

Even if there are bigger issues, smaller problems are still worth solving in their own right.

Practice Example

Imagine someone says, "We shouldn't worry about pollution here because other countries pollute more." While other places may have severe pollution, local pollution still matters and addressing it can make a difference.

Defending Against *Relative Privation*

When someone uses the Fallacy of *Relative Privation*, here's how to keep the discussion focused:

- **Acknowledge Other Problems but Return to the Topic**

    Say, "Yes, there are bigger issues, but this one still deserves attention."

- **Emphasize That Multiple Problems Can Be Addressed**

  Add, "We don't have to ignore smaller problems just because bigger ones exist."

- **Point Out That Problem Solving Isn't a Competition**

  Remind them, "Different issues matter in different ways, and solving one doesn't mean ignoring others."

By recognizing the Fallacy of *Relative Privation*, you'll approach problems with balance and perspective, acknowledging that multiple issues can matter at once. But sometimes, arguments shift from logic to pressure, using force rather than reason to sway others. Let's take a closer look at this next fallacy!

Chapter 43: The Appeal to Force Fallacy

The *Appeal to Force* fallacy, also known as *Argumentum ad* Baculum (Latin for "appeal to the stick"), occurs when someone tries to win an argument by using threats or intimidation instead of logic. It's like saying, "You'd better agree with me, or you'll regret it!" Here, the argument relies on fear rather than evidence, making it an unfair and manipulative tactic.

Why Is *Appeal to Force* a Fallacy?

The Appeal to Force is flawed because threats don't make a claim true or valid. Using intimidation to win an argument bypasses reason and relies on fear to silence opposition. In rational discussions, ideas should stand on their own merit, not on the perceived consequences.

Why Do Humans Use *Appeal to Force*?

Humans sometimes resort to this fallacy when they feel defensive or lack strong evidence to support their position. Using threats or intimidation can feel like an easy way to "win" the argument without actually providing support. Recognizing this fallacy helps us stand up for fair discussions and resist being swayed by fear tactics.

How to Avoid *Appeal to Force*

1. Focus on Evidence and Reasoning

When presenting an argument, ensure you're relying on facts and reasoning rather than emotions or pressure.

2. Avoid Intimidation Tactics

Don't rely on fear or threats to persuade others. Instead, explain why your position makes sense.

3. Encourage Open Dialogue

Make it clear that all viewpoints are welcome, and respect differing opinions.

Practice Example

Imagine someone says, "If you don't support this policy, you'll lose all my respect." This pressure doesn't make the policy any better; it's simply an attempt to force agreement without reasoning.

Defending Against *Appeal to Force*

When someone uses the *Appeal to Force* fallacy, here's how to respond assertively:

• Stand Up for Logic

Say, "I prefer to base my views on reasoning rather than pressure."

- **Request Evidence Instead of Intimidation**

  Suggest, "Let's look at the facts instead of relying on threats."

- **Encourage Respectful Discussion**

  Remind them, "We can disagree without needing to resort to threats or intimidation."

By recognizing the *Appeal to Force* fallacy, you'll make arguments based on logic, not fear, and encourage fair, respectful conversations. There's another persuasive trick to watch out for — one that swaps intimidation for excessive praise. Let's unpack this next fallacy.

Chapter 44: The Appeal to Flattery Fallacy

The *Appeal to Flattery* fallacy happens when someone uses compliments or flattery to persuade someone rather than presenting logical arguments. It's like saying, "You're so smart; I'm sure you'll agree with my idea!" Here, the argument is based on making the other person feel good, rather than using reason or evidence to convince them.

Why Is *Appeal to Flattery* a Fallacy?

The *Appeal to Flattery* is flawed because compliments don't make a claim true. While everyone enjoys feeling valued, praise shouldn't replace logic in an argument. For reasoning to be strong, it needs evidence — not just positive feelings.

Why Do Humans Use *Appeal to Flattery*?

Humans often use this fallacy because flattery can create goodwill, making others more inclined to agree. It's a shortcut to gaining support without the effort of presenting a well-reasoned argument. Recognizing this tactic helps us see past compliments to the real content of the argument.

How to Avoid *Appeal to Flattery*

1. Focus on Evidence, Not Emotions

Ask, "Am I agreeing because of the argument itself or because of how it makes me feel?"

2. Separate Compliments from Logic

Enjoy compliments, but don't let them cloud your judgment. An argument needs reasoning to stand strong.

3. Look for Substance in the Argument

Compliments are nice, but ask if there's real evidence backing up the claim.

Practice Example

Imagine someone says, "Only someone with great taste, like you, would support this idea!" Instead of being swayed by flattery, focus on the idea's strengths and weaknesses. Does it make sense on its own?

Defending Against *Appeal to Flattery*

When someone uses flattery in an argument, here's how to stay focused on facts:

• Thank Them, Then Focus on the Argument

Say, "I appreciate the compliment, but let's look at the reasoning behind it."

• Shift Attention Back to Evidence

Suggest, "What's the main reason you believe this? Let's focus on that."

• Separate Feelings from Facts

Gently remind them, "It's a nice compliment, but I need more than that to be convinced."

By recognizing the *Appeal to Flattery* fallacy, you'll make decisions based on reasoning rather than just nice words. But beware — some arguments rely on "common sense" to avoid deeper thinking.

Chapter 45: The Appeal to Common Sense Fallacy

The *Appeal to Common Sense* fallacy occurs when someone argues that a claim must be true because it's "common sense" or "obvious," rather than providing specific reasons or evidence. It's like saying, "It's just common sense that this policy will work—everyone knows it!" Here, the argument relies on the assumption that something is widely accepted, rather than on actual proof or explanation.

Why Is *Appeal to Common Sense* a Fallacy?

The *Appeal to Common Sense* is flawed because what seems like "common sense" can vary from person to person and isn't always accurate. Just because something feels obvious doesn't make it true. Sound arguments need clear reasoning and evidence, not just vague appeals.

Why Do Humans Use *Appeal to Common Sense*?

Humans often fall into this fallacy because "common sense" arguments feel simple and self-evident, making it easier to assume that others will automatically agree. It can be a shortcut to avoid providing actual evidence. Recognizing this tendency helps us stay grounded in proof rather than assumptions.

How to Avoid Appeal to Common Sense

1. Ask for Clarification

If someone says it's "common sense," ask, "What specifically makes this true?" This keeps the conversation focused on reasons.

2. Seek Real Evidence

Instead of accepting "obvious" ideas, look for solid evidence to support the claim.

3. Acknowledge That Common Sense Isn't Universal

Remember that common sense can mean different things to different people.

Practice Example

Imagine someone says, "It's common sense that kids learn best with strict discipline." Instead of accepting this at face value, ask, "What studies or evidence show that strict discipline improves learning?" This approach encourages a fact-based discussion.

Defending Against *Appeal to Common Sense*

When someone relies on "common sense" as their main argument, here's how to gently push for more substance:

• **Ask for Specifics**

Say, "What specific reasons support this idea?" This prompts them to clarify their argument.

- **Encourage Evidence Over Assumptions**

  Suggest, "Let's look at the evidence rather than assuming it's obvious."

- **Point Out That Common Sense Varies**

  Gently add, "What seems like common sense isn't always true or universal." This encourages a more open-minded approach.

By understanding the *Appeal to Common Sense* fallacy, you'll avoid assumptions and focus on specific reasons and facts. But there's another persuasive trick to watch out for — one that equates wealth with wisdom. Let's discuss this next fallacy.

Chapter 46: The Appeal to Wealth Fallacy

The *Appeal to Wealth* fallacy happens when someone assumes that something is better or more valuable simply because it's more expensive or associated with wealthy people. It's like saying, "This car is the best because it's the most expensive one available!" Here, the argument assumes that price or wealth equals quality, without examining other factors.

Why Is *Appeal to Wealth* a Fallacy?

The *Appeal to Wealth* is flawed because the cost or wealth associated with something doesn't necessarily reflect its quality or value. High prices can be based on branding or market factors, not on actual superiority. Rational thinking requires looking at the quality, performance, and actual benefits of something, not just its cost.

Why Do Humans Use *Appeal to Wealth*?

Humans often use this fallacy because wealth and high price tags can create a perception of luxury and excellence. This "halo effect" makes it easy to assume that expensive things are better, but recognizing this fallacy helps us evaluate products, ideas, and people based on actual merit.

How to Avoid *Appeal to Wealth*

1. Examine Quality Over Price

> Ask yourself, "Is this truly better, or am I assuming quality based on cost?"

2. Avoid Letting Price Cloud Judgment

> Just because something is expensive doesn't mean it's the best option.

3. Look for Value Rather Than Price

> Focus on the specific benefits, functionality, and quality of a product or idea, not just its cost.

Practice Example

Imagine someone says, "This skincare product is definitely the best because it's the most expensive one in the store." Instead of relying on the price tag alone, consider checking product reviews or ingredients to see if it actually meets your needs.

Defending Against *Appeal to Wealth*

When someone assumes something is better based on wealth, here's how to encourage a focus on quality:

- **Ask About Specific Qualities**

> Say, "What features or qualities make this the best choice, other than price?"

- **Shift Focus from Cost to Functionality**

  Suggest, "Let's look at how well it actually performs instead of the cost alone."

- **Point Out That Cost Doesn't Equal Quality**

  Gently remind them, "Price doesn't always reflect quality. Let's evaluate the actual benefits."

By understanding the *Appeal to Wealth* fallacy, you can evaluate things based on their true value rather than just their price tag. There's another trap that relies on credibility without accuracy — using sources or quotes in misleading ways. Let's take a closer look at this next fallacy.

Chapter 47: The False Attribution Fallacy

The *False* Attribution fallacy happens when someone references an unreliable or incorrect source to support their argument, often without verifying the source's credibility. It's like saying, "As Einstein once said, 'Imagination is more powerful than knowledge,'" without confirming that Einstein actually said this. In this fallacy, the argument is built on weak or false information.

Why Is *False Attribution* a Fallacy?

The *False Attribution* fallacy is flawed because a claim based on a fake or unreliable source can mislead people. Even if a source sounds authoritative, if it's not accurate or relevant, it doesn't add value to the argument. Strong arguments rely on trustworthy sources, not on famous names or random quotes.

Why Do Humans Use *False Attribution*?

Humans often fall into this fallacy because it's easy to assume that popular quotes or famous figures add credibility. Using a well-known name or authority can make arguments feel more persuasive, even if the source is misattributed or unreliable. Recognizing this fallacy helps us rely on accurate information.

How to Avoid *False Attribution*

1. Verify Sources Before Quoting

Before using a quote or reference, ask, "Is this source credible, and did they really say this?"

2. Look for Reliable Evidence

Instead of relying on popular quotes, find primary sources or verified statements to support your argument.

3. Be Cautious with Unverified Claims

Avoid using a source unless you're sure it's accurate and relevant.

Practice Example

Imagine someone says, "As Shakespeare once said, 'Love conquers all.'" While this sounds profound, it's actually a line from Virgil, not Shakespeare. Relying on misattributed quotes weakens the argument. A better approach is to double-check the source and find a relevant, reliable reference.

Defending Against *False Attribution*

When someone relies on a questionable source, here's how to guide them toward accurate information:

• Ask About the Source's Credibility

Say, "Is this a verified quote? Let's double-check to make sure it's accurate."

- **Suggest Finding a Reliable Source**

  Gently add, "Maybe we can find a source that's more credible to support this claim."

- **Encourage Using Primary or Trusted Sources**

  Remind them, "Strong arguments come from verified sources rather than random quotes."

By understanding the *False Attribution* fallacy, you'll rely on accurate sources, making your arguments stronger and more reliable. But sometimes, arguments confuse harm for progress, assuming that damage or loss can actually benefit the whole. Let's take a closer look at this next fallacy!

Chapter 48: The Broken Window Fallacy

The *Broken Window* Fallacy occurs when someone assumes that destruction or damage can have positive economic benefits by creating jobs or stimulating spending. It's like saying, "This broken window is good for the economy because it keeps glassmakers in business!" Here, the argument ignores the hidden costs and lost opportunities that come from replacing something that was already functioning.

Why Is *Broken Window* a Fallacy?

The *Broken Window* Fallacy is flawed because it only considers the immediate, visible benefits of repair without acknowledging the unseen costs. Fixing damage doesn't actually add value — it simply restores something to its previous state. Instead of using resources to build or improve, the resources are used to fix what was lost. True economic growth comes from creating new value, not from replacing what was destroyed.

Why Do Humans Use *Broken Window* Fallacy?

Humans often fall into this fallacy because the immediate benefits of repair are easy to see, while the hidden costs are less obvious. When something breaks, the visible repair process can make it seem as though new value is being added, but in reality, the resources could have been used for something more productive.

How to Avoid the *Broken Window* Fallacy

1. Consider the Full Economic Impact

Ask, "Are we creating new value, or are we just replacing what was lost?"

2. Think About Opportunity Costs

Recognize that money spent on repairs could have been used to create new benefits elsewhere.

3. Distinguish Between Restoring and Growing

Focus on activities that add value beyond merely fixing what was broken.

Practice Example

Imagine someone says, "Natural disasters are good for the economy because they create jobs in rebuilding." While rebuilding efforts can create jobs, they don't truly grow the economy. Resources are spent just to bring things back to normal instead of creating new value.

Defending Against *Broken Window* Fallacy

When someone assumes that destruction benefits the economy, here's how to highlight the unseen costs:

- **Point Out the Lost Opportunities**

Say, "What could those resources have achieved if they hadn't been used for repairs?"

- **Explain That Repair Doesn't Add New Value**
  Add, "Repairing damage doesn't improve the economy—it just brings things back to where they were."

- **Encourage Thinking About True Growth**
  Suggest, "Let's focus on ways to create value rather than just replacing what was lost."

By recognizing the *Broken Window* Fallacy, you'll see that economic growth requires creating new value, not just fixing what's broken. Great job! But there's another pitfall to watch for —one that involves projecting human traits onto non-human things. Let's explore this next fallacy!

Chapter 49: The Anthropomorphic Fallacy

The *Anthropomorphic* Fallacy happens when someone attributes human qualities, emotions, or intentions to non-human entities, such as animals, machines, or nature. It's like saying, "The weather is angry today!" or "My car hates me."

Why Is *Anthropomorphic* a Fallacy?

The *Anthropomorphic* Fallacy is flawed because it can lead to misunderstandings about the nature of non-human entities. While describing a storm as "angry" might be poetic, it doesn't accurately represent the reality of weather patterns, which aren't driven by emotions. Logical reasoning means understanding things as they are, not as we imagine them to be.

Why Do Humans Use *Anthropomorphic* Fallacy?

Humans naturally interpret the world through a human lens, which can make it easy to project our emotions or intentions onto other things. Anthropomorphism can help make sense of complex phenomena, but it can also lead to mistaken ideas, such as thinking that nature or machines have intentions.

How to Avoid the *Anthropomorphic* Fallacy

1. Recognize the Difference Between Human and Non-Human Entities

Remember that only humans (and certain animals) experience complex emotions and intentions.

2. Focus on Factual Descriptions

Describe things as they are, without adding human-like qualities.

3. Be Mindful of Figurative Language

While it's fine to use metaphors, make sure they don't distort your understanding of reality.

Practice Example

Imagine someone says, "This computer hates me! It always crashes when I'm working." The computer isn't capable of feelings or intentions. It's more accurate to say, "The computer is malfunctioning," which avoids attributing human motives to a machine.

Defending Against *Anthropomorphic* Fallacy

When someone attributes human traits to non-human things, here's how to bring the discussion back to reality:

• Encourage Realistic Descriptions

Say, "It might feel like the computer is against you, but it's just experiencing a technical issue."

- **Gently Separate Feelings from Facts**

  Suggest, "Let's look at this as a machine issue rather than a matter of intention."

- **Highlight That Non-Humans Don't Have Human Motives**

  Remind them, "Nature, machines, and animals don't have human emotions or motives like we do."

By recognizing the *Anthropomorphic* Fallacy, you'll interpret the world more accurately and avoid projecting human qualities onto non-human entities. However, sometimes, arguments hinge on surprise or disbelief — assuming something can't be true just because it seems astonishing. Let's explore this further.

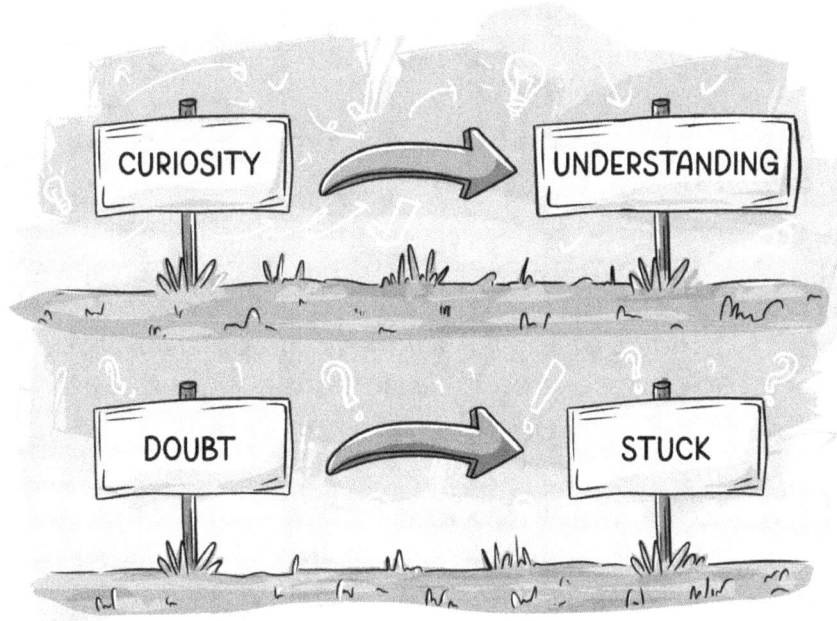

Chapter 50: The Argument from Personal Astonishment Fallacy

The *Argument from Personal Astonishment* (also called the Argument *from Incredulity*) occurs when someone argues that something must be false or impossible simply because they personally find it hard to believe. It's like saying, "I can't imagine how planes stay in the air, so there must be something suspicious going on with aviation." Here, the argument is based on a lack of understanding rather than on evidence or logic.

Why Is *Argument from Personal Astonishment* a Fallacy?

The *Argument from Personal Astonishment* is flawed because our personal understanding doesn't determine what's possible or true. Just because something seems confusing or complex doesn't mean it's false or invalid. In reality, some topics (such as science and technology) require specialized knowledge that isn't immediately obvious to everyone.

Why Do Humans Use *Argument from Personal Astonishment*?

Humans use this fallacy because we naturally rely on our personal experiences to make sense of the world. When something seems confusing, we may instinctively doubt it. Recognizing this fallacy helps us accept that things can be true even if we don't fully understand them.

How to Avoid *Argument from Personal Astonishment*

1. Acknowledge Knowledge Gaps

Accept that not understanding something doesn't make it untrue. Ask, "Could there be information I'm missing?"

2. Seek Evidence Rather Than Assumptions

Instead of dismissing something because it feels strange, look for reliable sources that explain it.

3. Stay Open to Complex Ideas

Recognize that many truths are complex. Be willing to learn rather than reject things outright.

Practice Example

Imagine someone says, "I can't believe humans evolved from simple organisms—it's just too strange to be true!" This is the *Argument from Personal Astonishment*. Instead, they could seek out scientific explanations for evolution rather than dismissing it based on initial disbelief.

Defending Against *Argument from Personal Astonishment*

When someone doubts something simply because they don't understand it, here's how to encourage open-mindedness:

- **Encourage Learning**

  Say, "Not understanding something doesn't mean it isn't true. Let's look at the evidence."

- **Point Out That Complexity Doesn't Equal Falsehood**

  Gently add, "Many things are complex, but that doesn't make them less real."

- **Suggest Research Instead of Rejection**

  Remind them, "Sometimes learning more can make things clearer."

By recognizing the *Argument from Personal Astonishment*, you'll be open to learning about complex ideas rather than rejecting them out of disbelief. But sometimes, arguments lean on the idea that if "everyone" believes it, it must be true. Let's unpack this next.

Chapter 51: The Appeal to Wisdom of the Crowd Fallacy

The *Appeal to Wisdom of the Crowd* fallacy, also known as the *Bandwagon of Belief*, occurs when someone assumes that a belief must be true simply because it's widely held by a large group. It's like saying, "Most people think this brand of shoes is the best, so it must be true!" Here, the argument relies on popularity rather than on actual evidence.

Why Is *Appeal to Wisdom of the Crowd* a Fallacy?

The *Appeal to Wisdom of the Crowd* is flawed because popularity doesn't determine truth. Just because many people believe something doesn't make it accurate. Good reasoning requires looking at facts and evidence rather than following the majority opinion, which can sometimes be based on trends, misinformation, or assumptions.

Why Do Humans Use *Appeal to Wisdom of the Crowd*?

Humans often rely on this fallacy because following the crowd feels comfortable and reassuring. It's easy to assume that if many people believe something, it must be true. Recognizing this tendency helps us focus on reliable information.

How to Avoid the *Appeal to Wisdom of the Crowd*

1. Look for Evidence Beyond Popularity

Ask, "Is there real evidence supporting this, or just a lot of people who believe it?"

2. Avoid Assuming Truth from Belief Numbers

Recognize that even widely accepted ideas need factual support to be valid.

3. Focus on Facts, Not Fads

Distinguish between what's truly supported by evidence and what's just a popular belief.

Practice Example

Imagine someone says, "Everyone says this diet is the best, so it has to be true!" Instead of relying on popularity, a better approach would be to research studies and results that objectively support the diet's effectiveness.

Defending Against *Appeal to Wisdom of the Crowd*

When someone relies on popular belief to argue a point, here's how to refocus on evidence:

- #### Ask About Evidence Supporting the Belief

Say, "What specific evidence shows this belief is true?"

- #### Point Out That Popularity Isn't Proof

Gently add, "Just because many people believe it doesn't mean it's accurate."

- **Encourage Independent Research**

  Suggest, "Let's look at the data to see if it really holds up."

By recognizing the *Appeal to Wisdom of the Crowd*, you'll make choices based on solid evidence rather than simply going with the flow. But sometimes, an argument relies on something's age rather than its actual value, suggesting it's correct just because it's old. Let's unpack this next fallacy.

Chapter 52: The Appeal to Antiquity Fallacy

The *Appeal to Antiquity* fallacy, also known as the *Appeal to Tradition*, occurs when someone argues that something must be right or better simply because it's been done for a long time. It's like saying, "This is the best way to do it because that's how our ancestors did it." Here, the argument relies on tradition as proof of value or truth, rather than on evidence.

Why Is *Appeal to Antiquity* a Fallacy?

The *Appeal to Antiquity* is flawed because if something has been done a certain way for a long time, it doesn't mean it's the best or only way. New ideas and approaches can often improve on traditions. Rational thinking means evaluating methods based on effectiveness.

Why Do Humans Use *Appeal to Antiquity*?

Humans often use this fallacy because they find comfort in tradition. What's familiar feels reliable and safe, making it tempting to assume that long-standing practices must be best. Recognizing this tendency helps us evaluate practices on their merits.

How to Avoid the *Appeal to Antiquity*

1. Focus on Effectiveness, Not Just Age

Ask, "Is this method the best, or just the oldest?"

2. Consider Alternatives with an Open Mind

Be willing to explore new ideas and techniques that might improve on tradition.

3. Evaluate Tradition's Benefits and Drawbacks

Acknowledge that while traditions can be valuable, they still need to be examined for current relevance.

Practice Example

Imagine someone says, "Our company should continue using paper files because that's how it's always been done." Instead of relying on tradition, it's more logical to consider if digital files might be more efficient and environmentally friendly.

Defending Against *Appeal to Antiquity*

When someone insists on a method based on tradition, here's how to bring the discussion back to practical value:

- #### Ask About Modern Benefits

  Say, "Does this method still work best, or are there better ways now?"

- #### Encourage Evaluating Tradition's Relevance

  Gently add, "Tradition has value, but let's see if it's still effective for today."

- **Suggest Considering Alternatives**
  Remind them, "Sometimes newer ideas improve on what's been done before."

By recognizing the *Appeal to Antiquity* fallacy, you value methods based on usefulness, not just history. But there's another trap to watch out for — one that leads people to overvalue immediate rewards over future benefits.

Chapter 53: The Hyperbolic Discounting Fallacy

The *Hyperbolic Discounting* fallacy occurs when someone places more value on immediate rewards over larger, future rewards. It's like saying, "I'd rather have $20 right now than wait a year for $100!" Here, the decision is driven by the desire for instant gratification, even if waiting would lead to a better outcome.

Why Is *Hyperbolic Discounting* a Fallacy?

The *Hyperbolic Discounting* fallacy is flawed because it ignores the long-term benefits of patience and overvalues immediate rewards. Rational decision-making requires weighing both short-term and long-term outcomes.

Why Do Humans Use *Hyperbolic Discounting*?

Humans often use this fallacy because our brains are wired to prefer immediate rewards over delayed ones, even when waiting would lead to greater benefits. Recognizing this tendency helps us make decisions that balance present desires with future gains.

How to Avoid *Hyperbolic Discounting*

1. Compare Immediate Gains with Long-Term Benefits

Ask yourself, "Will waiting lead to a better outcome than taking the reward now?"

2. Think About Future Consequences

Consider how taking an instant reward might limit your options or benefits in the future.

3. Practice Patience in Decision-Making

Get comfortable with delayed rewards by setting goals and focusing on long-term benefits.

Practice Example

Imagine someone says, "I'd rather spend my savings on a new gadget now than invest it for retirement." While spending brings immediate pleasure, investing may lead to much greater security and satisfaction in the future.

Defending Against *Hyperbolic Discounting*

When someone is focused on immediate rewards over future gains, here's how to encourage long-term thinking:

• Highlight the Value of Waiting

Say, "Sometimes, waiting brings greater rewards in the future."

• Encourage Looking at Future Benefits

Suggest, "Let's consider how this decision could benefit you later on."

• Point Out Potential Long-Term Gains

Remind them, "Immediate rewards can feel good, but future gains might be worth the wait."

By recognizing the *Hyperbolic Discounting* fallacy, you can make choices that consider both present and future benefits, leading to wiser long-term decisions. Sometimes, however, an argument gives two sides equal weight, even when one lacks real evidence. Let's explore this next fallacy!

Chapter 54: The False Balance Fallacy

The *False Balance* fallacy happens when someone treats two sides of an argument as if they are equally valid, even when one side is clearly stronger or more credible. It's like saying, "Scientists say climate change is real, but some people disagree, so both sides must have equal merit." Here, the argument gives an illusion of fairness, but it misrepresents the strength of each position.

Why Is *False Balance* a Fallacy?

The *False Balance* fallacy is flawed because it ignores the weight of evidence on each side. Not all arguments or sources are equally credible; some are backed by extensive research, while others are based on anecdote or opinion. Rational thinking requires recognizing when one side has more evidence or expertise supporting it.

Why Do Humans Use False Balance?

Humans often fall into this fallacy because we're taught to respect all perspectives. While this is a valuable principle, it can sometimes lead to the mistaken belief that all views are equally valid, even if one side lacks strong support. Recognizing this tendency helps us weigh arguments based on merit rather than striving for artificial balance.

How to Avoid *False Balance*

1. Evaluate Each Side's Evidence

Ask yourself, "Does each side have equal evidence, or is one side stronger?"

2. Recognize Expertise and Consensus

Consider the sources and their credibility—experts with data and research should weigh more than opinions without evidence.

3. Distinguish Between Balance and Accuracy

Sometimes, an accurate conclusion doesn't mean giving equal weight to every perspective.

Practice Example

Imagine someone says, "Some people say vaccines are safe, and others disagree, so both sides should be treated equally." While it's important to listen, scientific research overwhelmingly supports vaccine safety. A balanced presentation would focus on the weight of evidence rather than treating each view as equal.

Defending Against *False Balance*

When someone tries to give equal weight to both sides of an uneven argument, here's how to help them focus on credibility:

- ### Ask About the Evidence for Each Side

  Say, "Is there strong evidence supporting both sides, or is one side better supported?"

• Point Out When There's Consensus

Suggest, "Sometimes, there's a clear majority of evidence that should weigh more."

• Emphasize Expertise Over Opinion

Remind them, "Not all sources have the same credibility. Let's focus on those with the strongest evidence."

By recognizing the *False Balance* fallacy, you can avoid giving undue weight to unsupported views and focus on the strength of evidence. Be careful, though — sometimes, arguments use fear to sway opinion rather than relying on facts, as we explain next.

Chapter 55: The Appeal to Fear Fallacy

The *Appeal to Fear* fallacy happens when someone tries to persuade by creating fear instead of providing logical reasons. It's like saying, "If you don't buy this insurance, you'll regret it when disaster strikes!" Here, the argument relies on scaring people rather than using facts to make a strong case.

Why *Is Appeal to Fear* a Fallacy?

The *Appeal to Fear* is flawed because fear alone doesn't prove a point. While fear can be a powerful motivator, it doesn't provide any evidence that a claim is true. Good reasoning is based on logic and facts, not just emotions. Relying on fear can lead people to make irrational choices that they might otherwise avoid.

Why Do Humans Use *Appeal to Fear*?

Humans often respond strongly to fear because it's a basic survival instinct. Appeals to fear can feel persuasive because they trigger an emotional response, but they often bypass rational thinking. Recognizing this fallacy helps us stay grounded in reason, even in situations that provoke strong emotions.

How to Avoid the *Appeal to Fear*

1. Focus on Facts Over Feelings

Ask yourself, "Is this argument based on evidence, or just fear?"

2. Seek Evidence to Support the Claim

If something sounds scary, look for data that backs it up rather than just reacting to the emotion.

3. Pause to Evaluate Before Responding

Give yourself time to assess whether fear is clouding your judgment.

Practice Example

Imagine someone says, "If you don't support this policy, crime will skyrocket, and everyone will be in danger!" Instead of being swayed by fear, a more rational approach would be to examine crime statistics and assess whether the policy truly addresses safety.

Defending Against *Appeal to Fear*

When someone uses fear instead of logic, here's how to stay focused on facts:

• Ask for Factual Support

Say, "Can we look at the data supporting this claim instead of just worrying?"

• Point Out the Need for Evidence Over Emotion

Gently add, "Fear alone doesn't prove anything. Let's examine the facts."

- **Encourage Calm, Rational Thinking**

  Suggest, "Let's consider this logically instead of focusing on worst-case scenarios."

By understanding the *Appeal to Fear* fallacy, you'll make decisions based on reason rather than on worry or alarm. But sometimes, arguments assume that the middle ground is always the best solution, even when it isn't. Let's explore this next fallacy!

Chapter 56: The Argument to Moderation Fallacy

The *Argument to Moderation* fallacy, also known as the *False Compromise* or *Middle Ground Fallacy*, occurs when someone assumes that the best solution must be a compromise between two opposing viewpoints. It's like saying, "Some people think the earth is round, others think it's flat—so it must be somewhere in between." Here, the argument relies on the idea that the truth lies halfway between extremes, rather than where the evidence points.

Why Is *Argument to Moderation* a Fallacy?

The *Argument to Moderation* is flawed because the truth isn't always in the middle. Sometimes one side is clearly correct, while the other is based on faulty reasoning. Compromising between two views doesn't automatically make a solution fair or accurate — good reasoning requires evaluating the merits of each position.

Why Do Humans Use Argument to Moderation?

Humans often fall into this fallacy because compromise feels fair and non-confrontational. It's tempting to think that agreeing somewhere in the middle is the most reasonable approach. However, recognizing this fallacy helps us see that some arguments have clear evidence on one side, and compromise isn't always the answer.

How to Avoid *Argument to Moderation*

1. Evaluate Evidence for Each Side

Ask yourself, "Does the evidence support one side more than the other, or does it truly lie somewhere in between?"

2. Avoid Assuming Compromise Equals Fairness

Just because a solution is in the middle doesn't mean it's accurate or just.

3. Consider Each Argument Separately

Focus on the strengths and weaknesses of each position instead of forcing a middle ground.

Practice Example

Imagine someone says, "Some people say vaccines are safe, others say they're dangerous, so they must be somewhere in between." Here, treating vaccine safety as a compromise between "safe" and "unsafe" ignores overwhelming scientific evidence supporting their safety.

Defending Against *Argument to Moderation*

When someone tries to find a compromise where none is needed, here's how to bring them back to evidence:

- ### Ask About the Supporting Evidence

  Say, "Does the evidence really support a compromise, or is one side stronger?"

- **Point Out When One Side Is Well-Researched**

Gently add, "Sometimes, the facts clearly support one side over the other."

- **Emphasize That Fairness and Accuracy Aren't Always the Same**

Suggest, "True fairness means going where the evidence leads, not just compromising."

By recognizing the *Argument to Moderation*, you'll understand that the best answer isn't always in the middle — it's wherever the evidence leads. However, arguments sometimes rely on the authority of past figures, assuming their wisdom applies universally. Let's take a closer look at this next fallacy!

Chapter 57: The Appeal to Authority of the Past Fallacy

The *Appeal to Authority of the Past* fallacy occurs when someone insists that an idea or belief is correct simply because it was endorsed by a well-known figure or authority from history. It's like saying, "Aristotle believed this, so it must be true today." Here, the argument relies on historical authority rather than evaluating current evidence.

Why Is *Appeal to Authority of the Past* a Fallacy?

The *Appeal to Authority of the Past* is flawed because even the greatest thinkers of the past didn't have access to all the knowledge we have today. While historical figures contributed valuable ideas, they were still limited by the science and understanding of their time. Strong reasoning looks at current evidence and methods rather than relying solely on tradition or historical authority.

Why Do Humans Use *Appeal to Authority of the Past?*

Humans often fall into this fallacy because historical figures like Aristotle, Plato, or Newton are widely respected. Quoting them can make arguments feel persuasive or trustworthy. Recognizing this tendency helps us focus on current evidence, rather than assuming that something is right just because it was believed long ago.

How to Avoid *Appeal to Authority of the Past*

1. Check for Modern Evidence

Ask yourself, "Is this claim still supported by current research, or is it just based on tradition?"

2. Recognize the Limits of Historical Knowledge

Historical figures did the best they could with what they knew, but science and knowledge have advanced.

3. Evaluate Ideas Based on Today's Understanding

Focus on present-day research and understanding, especially in fields that have evolved significantly.

Practice Example

Imagine someone says, "Ancient philosophers believed in spontaneous generation, so it must have some truth to it." While this idea was common historically, modern biology disproves it. Instead of relying on past authority, it's better to look at the evidence provided by current science.

Defending Against *Appeal to Authority of the Past*

When someone relies on historical authority to argue a point, here's how to encourage an evidence-based approach:

- **Ask About Current Evidence**

Say, "Do we have modern research that supports this idea?"

- **Point Out Advances in Knowledge**

Gently add, "Science has progressed since then, so we may know more now than they did."

- **Encourage Looking Forward Instead of Backward**

Remind them, "While historical figures made important contributions, we have new knowledge they didn't have."

By recognizing the *Appeal to Authority of the Past*, you'll focus on the latest, most accurate information rather than on the limitations of historical knowledge. Excellent work — each fallacy you understand makes your reasoning sharper and more evidence-based! But there's another trap to watch out for — the assumption that the world is always fair and that people always get what they deserve. Let's explore this next.

Chapter 58: The Just-World Fallacy

The *Just-World* Fallacy occurs when someone assumes that good things happen to good people and bad things happen to bad people because the world is inherently fair. It's like saying, "If someone is poor, they must not have worked hard enough." This fallacy assumes that everyone gets what they deserve, ignoring other factors that affect outcomes.

Why Is *Just-World* a Fallacy?

The *Just-World* Fallacy is flawed because it oversimplifies complex situations and doesn't account for the role of luck, inequality, and external factors. While it can be comforting to believe in a fair world, real life is more complicated, and people's outcomes are influenced by many forces beyond their control. Rational thinking requires understanding the complexities of cause and effect, not assuming fairness.

Why Do Humans Use the *Just-World* Fallacy?

Humans often fall into this fallacy because believing in a fair world feels reassuring. It's comforting to think that we can control our fate by making good choices, and that misfortune only happens to those who "deserve" it. Recognizing this tendency helps us empathize with others and acknowledge that life doesn't always follow a moral balance sheet.

How to Avoid the *Just-World* Fallacy

1. Recognize That Life Is Complex

Understand that many factors—like chance, privilege, and circumstance—affect people's lives.

2. Practice Empathy Over Judgment

Instead of assuming someone's situation reflects their character, consider external factors they might face.

3. Acknowledge the Role of Randomness

Accept that both good and bad things can happen unpredictably and aren't always deserved.

Practice Example

Imagine someone says, "If they're in trouble, they must have done something to deserve it." This is the *Just-World Fallacy*. A more balanced approach would consider other factors, like luck, external circumstances, or systemic issues, that could contribute to someone's challenges.

Defending Against the *Just-World* Fallacy

When someone assumes that life is always fair, here's how to encourage them to consider other perspectives:

- **Point Out Complex Causes**

  Say, "Life isn't always fair, and many things are beyond our control."

- **Encourage Empathy**

  Suggest, "Sometimes people face challenges that aren't their fault. Let's look at the bigger picture."

- **Remind Them That Good and Bad Happen Randomly**

  Gently add, "Both fortune and misfortune can happen to anyone, regardless of their actions."

By recognizing the *Just-World* Fallacy, you'll approach situations with empathy and an understanding of life's complexities. Do beware — sometimes arguments rely on authority figures who aren't relevant to the topic, as we explain next.

Chapter 59: The Appeal to Irrelevant Authority Fallacy

The *Appeal to Irrelevant Authority* fallacy happens when someone supports a claim by citing an authority figure who isn't actually an expert on the topic. It's like saying, "This famous actor says this new diet works, so it must be true." Here, the argument relies on authority without checking if that authority is relevant.

Why Is *Appeal to Irrelevant Authority* a Fallacy?

The *Appeal to Irrelevant Authority* is flawed because expertise in one field doesn't mean expertise in another. Just because someone is respected or well-known doesn't mean they're qualified to speak on all topics. Sound reasoning means seeking information from credible sources who are knowledgeable in the specific area being discussed.

Why Do Humans Use *Appeal to Irrelevant Authority*?

Humans often use this fallacy because we're naturally influenced by people we admire or respect, even if their authority doesn't extend to the topic at hand. Recognizing this tendency helps us remember that true expertise is specific, not general, and even well-known figures can be mistaken outside their field.

How to Avoid *Appeal to Irrelevant Authority*

1. Check the Source's Expertise

Ask yourself, "Is this person truly an expert in this area, or just a well-known figure?"

2. Seek Field-Specific Knowledge

Rely on sources with proven expertise in the specific topic you're researching.

3. Recognize the Limits of Fame

Being famous doesn't make someone knowledgeable on every subject.

Practice Example

Imagine someone says, "A professional athlete recommends this investment strategy, so it must be effective." This is the *Appeal to Irrelevant Authority*. A more logical approach would be to consult financial experts who have specialized knowledge in investing.

Defending Against *Appeal to Irrelevant Authority*

When someone relies on an irrelevant authority to argue a point, here's how to guide them toward credible sources:

- **Ask About the Source's Credentials**

Say, "Is this person actually an expert in this field?"

- **Encourage Seeking Qualified Opinions**

Suggest, "Let's find information from someone with expertise in this specific area."

- **Point Out That Popularity Doesn't Equal Knowledge**
  Remind them, "Being well-known doesn't make someone an authority on every topic."

By recognizing the *Appeal to Irrelevant Authority*, you'll trust information from qualified experts rather than relying on fame or unrelated authority. But there's another trap to be aware of — assuming that controlled models can perfectly predict real-life situations. Let's explore this next fallacy.

Chapter 60: The Ludic Fallacy

The *Ludic Fallacy* happens when someone assumes that real-life situations work like controlled games or simplified models, where all the variables are predictable. It's like saying, "If I understand the rules of poker, I can predict how real-life risks work." Here, the fallacy relies on the mistaken belief that the messy, unpredictable nature of real life can be fully captured by neat, simplified rules.

Why Is *Ludic* a Fallacy?

The *Ludic Fallacy* is flawed because real life is far more complex and unpredictable than any game or model. Simplified systems often don't account for unexpected factors, hidden variables, or "unknown unknowns" that can affect outcomes. Sound reasoning means understanding that while models can be helpful, they don't capture all the complexities of real-world situations.

Why Do Humans Use the *Ludic* Fallacy?

Humans often fall into this fallacy because simplified models and games feel easy to understand and reassuring. We like rules and predictability, but life doesn't always follow neat patterns. Recognizing this fallacy helps us accept and prepare for the uncertainty and unpredictability of real-life events.

How to Avoid the *Ludic* Fallacy

1. Recognize Real-Life Complexity

Understand that life often involves factors that are hard to predict or account for.

2. Use Models as Guides, Not Absolutes

Models can be useful for learning, but they don't capture everything. Treat them as tools, not as perfect reflections of reality.

3. Stay Open to Surprises and Unknowns

Expect that real-world outcomes may differ from simplified predictions.

Practice Example

Imagine someone says, "If I can beat this strategy game, I'll have no problem navigating real-life business risks." This is the *Ludic* Fallacy—real business situations involve unpredictable factors like market changes, human behavior, and economic trends that can't always be modeled.

Defending Against the *Ludic* Fallacy

When someone assumes real life will follow the neat rules of a model, here's how to remind them of real-world complexity:

• Point Out Real-World Variables

Say, "Games and models don't always account for unexpected events or unknowns."

- **Encourage Real-World Testing**

  Suggest, "Let's see how this approach holds up in actual situations before assuming it's foolproof."

- **Remind Them That Models Are Simplified**

  Gently add, "Models can be helpful, but life is often messier than any set of rules."

By recognizing the *Ludic* Fallacy, you'll stay grounded in the complexity of reality and avoid relying too heavily on simplified rules. But sometimes, arguments assume that anything new must be better. Let's explore this topic next.

Chapter 61: The Pro-Innovation Bias Fallacy

The *Pro-Innovation Bias* Fallacy happens when someone assumes that a new idea, product, or technology is inherently better just because it's new. It's like saying, "This new app must be the best solution because it's based on the latest technology!" Here, the argument relies on novelty as proof of quality or improvement, rather than evaluating the actual effectiveness or value of the innovation.

Why Is *Pro-Innovation Bias* a Fallacy?

The *Pro-Innovation Bias* is flawed because "new" doesn't always mean "improved". Some innovations may add complexity without adding real value or may create unintended side effects. Rational thinking requires assessing each new idea on its practical benefits and drawbacks, rather than assuming it's better simply because it's different from what came before.

Why Do Humans Use *Pro-Innovation Bias*?

Humans often fall into this fallacy because they associate newness with progress and improvement. We're naturally drawn to novelty and tend to believe that change is always positive. Recognizing this tendency helps us approach innovation with a balanced view, rather than blindly following trends.

How to Avoid *Pro-Innovation Bias*

1. Evaluate the Practical Benefits

Ask yourself, "Does this new thing solve a real problem, or is it change for the sake of change?"

2. Consider Potential Downsides

Recognize that some innovations may introduce new issues or be less effective than previous solutions.

3. Focus on Value, Not Novelty

Assess whether the innovation truly improves on what came before, based on evidence rather than excitement.

Practice Example

Imagine someone says, "This new software update will definitely make things easier." While updates can improve functionality, they can also introduce bugs or complicated features. A more balanced approach would be to wait for reviews or test it to see if it actually adds value.

Defending Against *Pro-Innovation Bias*

When someone assumes that new is automatically better, here's how to encourage a focus on value:

- **Ask About Practical Benefits**

Say, "What specific improvements does this new idea or product offer?"

- **Encourage Testing and Evaluation**

Suggest, "Let's see if this innovation is truly effective before assuming it's better."

- **Point Out That Novelty Doesn't Guarantee Quality**

Gently add, "Just because it's new doesn't mean it's the best option."

By recognizing the *Pro-Innovation Bias*, you'll approach new ideas and technologies with curiosity but without assuming they're inherently superior. Remember, though, positive impressions in one area can lead to overestimations in others. Let's unpack this next fallacy!

Chapter 62: The Halo Effect Fallacy

The *Halo Effect* Fallacy happens when someone assumes that because a person or thing is good in one area, they must be good in other, unrelated areas as well. It's like saying, "This actor is talented, so their political opinions must be correct." Here, the argument relies on one positive trait to form an overall positive impression.

Why Is the *Halo Effect* a Fallacy?

The *Halo Effect* is flawed because expertise or talent in one area doesn't guarantee knowledge or quality in other areas. Rational thinking means evaluating each characteristic or quality separately. Just because someone excels in one domain doesn't mean they're qualified or credible in every area.

Why Do Humans Use the *Halo Effect?*

Humans use this fallacy because positive impressions are powerful, and it's natural to assume that someone who is skilled or likable in one way is generally admirable. This cognitive shortcut can save mental effort, but it often leads to uncritical acceptance of opinions or actions outside someone's area of expertise.

How to Avoid the *Halo Effect*

1. Judge Each Area Separately

Ask yourself, "Does this person's skill or quality in one area actually apply to this other area?"

2. Consider Relevant Expertise

Focus on whether someone's credibility or talent is relevant to the specific issue at hand.

3. Stay Aware of Biases

Acknowledge that admiration or respect in one area can cloud judgment in unrelated fields.

Practice Example

Imagine someone says, "This CEO runs a successful company, so their book on personal relationships must be excellent." Here, success in business doesn't necessarily mean expertise in relationships. A more critical approach would be to evaluate the book separately, without assuming it's credible based on the author's business background.

Defending Against the *Halo Effect*

When someone uses the *Halo Effect*, here's how to bring focus back to relevant qualities:

• Ask About Relevant Expertise

Say, "Is this skill relevant to the area we're discussing?"

- **Encourage Independent Evaluation**

  Suggest, "Let's evaluate this area on its own merits, without letting other qualities sway us."

- **Point Out That One Strength Doesn't Equal Total Expertise**

  Gently remind them, "Being skilled in one area doesn't guarantee knowledge in another."

By recognizing the *Halo Effect*, you'll make more accurate judgments based on relevant qualities rather than letting one good impression sway unrelated areas. Excellent work — each fallacy you learn adds precision to your reasoning! But there's another common trap to watch for — one that causes us to underestimate the time and effort needed for a task.

Chapter 63: The Planning Fallacy

The *Planning Fallacy* happens when someone underestimates the time, cost, or effort required to complete a task or project, often because they're overly optimistic. It's like saying, "I'll definitely finish this big project in two days," even though similar projects have taken a week in the past. Here, the argument relies on an overly positive outlook rather than on realistic expectations.

Why Is This a Fallacy?

The *Planning Fallacy* is flawed because it ignores past experiences and typical obstacles. People often assume they'll complete tasks quickly and smoothly, even when previous experiences suggest otherwise. Sound reasoning involves considering potential challenges and basing expectations on realistic timelines, not just best-case scenarios.

Why Do Humans Use the *Planning Fallacy?*

Humans fall into the *Planning Fallacy* because they're naturally optimistic about future events, often overlooking possible setbacks or challenges. They like to believe that everything will go smoothly, but recognizing this tendency helps them prepare for real-life complexities and avoid the disappointment of unmet expectations.

How to Avoid the *Planning Fallacy*

1. Base Plans on Past Experiences

Ask yourself, "How long did similar tasks take in the past? What challenges did I face?"

2. Account for Potential Setbacks

Assume that unexpected delays or issues might arise and build extra time into your plans.

3. Use Data and Realistic Projections

Make estimates based on data, rather than assuming an ideal outcome.

Practice Example

Imagine someone says, "This home renovation will be done in two weeks!" This is likely the *Planning Fallacy*, especially if past renovations have taken longer. A more realistic approach would be to look at average renovation times, include a buffer for potential delays, and expect that things might take longer than planned.

Defending Against the *Planning Fallacy*

When someone underestimates the time or effort required for a task, here's how to encourage realistic expectations:

• Ask About Similar Experiences

Say, "How long did similar projects take, and what challenges did you face?"

- **Encourage Including Extra Time**

  Suggest, "It's a good idea to build in some extra time in case of delays."

- **Remind Them That Optimism Isn't Always Realistic**

  Gently add, "Sometimes things take longer than we hope. Planning for that can save stress."

By recognizing the *Planning Fallacy*, you'll set more achievable goals and timelines, making it easier to meet deadlines and avoid disappointment. However, mistaken identity and assumptions can sometimes lead to errors in reasoning. Let's get into this next fallacy!

DIFFERENT LABELS, SAME IDENTITY.

Chapter 64: The Masked Man Fallacy

The *Masked Man* Fallacy occurs when someone assumes that if they know something about an object or person under one description, it must hold true under another, distinct description. For example, "I know Superman can fly, but I don't know that Clark Kent can fly, so Clark Kent isn't Superman." Here, different labels (or contexts) lead to the mistaken belief that two names or descriptions must refer to different things, even if they're actually the same.

Why Is the *Masked Man* a Fallacy?

The *Masked Man* Fallacy is flawed because it confuses identity with how something is described. In logic, if two names or descriptions refer to the same entity, the characteristics apply regardless of which label is used. Sound reasoning means recognizing that different ways of identifying something don't change the entity itself.

Why Do Humans Use the *Masked Man* Fallacy?

Humans often fall into this fallacy because different labels or appearances can influence how they think about something. This fallacy can also arise when people are unaware of all the facts and assume that different descriptions must refer to different things. Recognizing this tendency helps us see through surface differences to the underlying reality.

How to Avoid the *Masked Man* Fallacy

1. Focus on the Entity Itself

Ask yourself, "Do these different descriptions refer to the same thing, just in different contexts?"

2. Consider All Known Information

Make sure you have enough context to understand whether two labels might apply to one entity.

3. Avoid Assuming Different Labels Mean Different Things

Remember that names or contexts can change, but identity stays constant.

Practice Example

Imagine someone says, "I know Batman fights crime, but I don't know Bruce Wayne fights crime, so Batman can't be Bruce Wayne." This is the *Masked Man* Fallacy. Just because Bruce Wayne and Batman are different descriptions doesn't mean they refer to different people; they're simply different labels for the same individual.

Defending Against the *Masked Man* Fallacy

When someone assumes that two different descriptions mean different entities, here's how to bring the focus back to identity:

- **Ask About the Underlying Identity**

  Say, "Do these descriptions refer to the same thing, just in different contexts?"

- **Point Out that Labels Don't Change Essence**

  Gently add, "Different names don't change the underlying identity."

- **Encourage Thinking Beyond Appearances**

  Suggest, "Just because they look different doesn't mean they're separate entities."

By recognizing the *Masked Man* Fallacy, you'll be able to look beyond labels and appearances to understand the true identity of things. But beware — some arguments are crafted to be unbreakable, designed to deflect any challenge. Let's explore this next fallacy!

Chapter 65: The Self-Sealing Fallacy

The *Self-Sealing* Fallacy happens when someone makes a claim that's impossible to disprove because any counter-argument or evidence against it is automatically rejected or reinterpreted to fit the claim. It's like saying, "Everyone who disagrees with me is just too brainwashed to see the truth." Here, the argument is constructed so that it protects itself against any criticism, creating a "self-sealing" defense that makes it immune to outside scrutiny.

Why Is *Self-Sealing* a Fallacy?

The *Self-Sealing* Fallacy is flawed because it makes a claim unfalsifiable — no matter what evidence is presented, the claim is redefined or explained away to prevent any possibility of being proven wrong. Sound reasoning requires openness to evidence, even if it goes against the initial belief. If a claim can't be disproven in any scenario, it's not a testable or logical argument.

Why Do Humans Use the *Self-Sealing* Fallacy?

Humans often fall into this fallacy because it feels safer to hold onto beliefs that can't be challenged. By making arguments immune to counter-evidence, they avoid facing difficult questions or changing their minds. Recognizing this tendency helps us remain open to information that might challenge our views and keep our thinking flexible.

How to Avoid the *Self-Sealing* Fallacy

1. Stay Open to Counter-Evidence

Ask yourself, "What evidence would I accept as a reason to rethink my claim?"

2. Avoid Reinterpreting All Evidence to Fit the Argument

Allow counter-evidence to exist rather than immediately twisting it to support your position.

3. Test Claims Honestly

Think about how to evaluate your claim in a way that doesn't automatically reject opposing views.

Practice Example

Imagine someone says, "If you don't believe in my theory, it's because you haven't awakened to the truth." This is the Self-Sealing Fallacy because disagreement is explained as evidence of ignorance, rather than as a valid challenge to the theory. A more open-minded approach would allow others to disagree and explore whether the claim can stand up to criticism.

Defending Against the *Self-Sealing* Fallacy

When someone creates an argument that blocks all counterpoints, here's how to help them consider alternative views:

- **Ask What Would Change Their Mind**

  Say, "Is there any evidence that would make you reconsider this belief?"

- **Encourage Openness to Disagreement**

  Gently add, "Allowing counterpoints can help test if an argument is strong or needs adjusting."

- **Point Out That Unfalsifiable Claims Aren't Logical**

  Remind them, "If a claim can't be challenged, it can't be truly tested."

By recognizing the *Self-Sealing* Fallacy, you'll keep your arguments open to evidence and avoid creating unchallengeable beliefs. But there's another subtle trap to avoid — one that dismisses arguments based on suspected motives rather than engaging with the actual content. Let's discover more about this next fallacy.

Chapter 66: The Appeal to Motive Fallacy

The *Appeal to Motive* Fallacy happens when someone dismisses an argument by questioning the motives behind it, instead of addressing the argument's actual content. It's like saying, "You're only supporting this policy because you'll benefit from it, so it must be wrong." Here, the focus is on the person's possible motivations, rather than the validity of what they're saying.

Why Is *Appeal to Motive* a Fallacy?

The *Appeal to Motive* is flawed because even if someone has a personal reason for making a claim, it doesn't automatically make the claim false. Dismissing an argument based on motives ignores the actual evidence or reasoning behind it. Sound reasoning requires analyzing the argument itself, not just the possible interests of the person presenting it.

Why Do Humans Use the *Appeal to Motive* Fallacy?

Humans often fall into this fallacy because questioning motives can seem like an easy way to discredit someone's stance. It can feel satisfying to assume that people are biased or self-serving, but this doesn't address the actual quality of their argument. Recognizing this tendency helps us focus on facts and evidence, rather than personal suspicions.

How to Avoid the *Appeal to Motive* Fallacy

1. Focus on the Argument's Content

Ask yourself, "Is there valid reasoning or evidence in their argument, regardless of their motives?"

2. Acknowledge That Motives and Truth Aren't Linked

Remember that even if someone stands to benefit, it doesn't mean their argument is invalid.

3. Separate the Person from the Argument

Evaluate the argument on its own merits, rather than making assumptions about the person presenting it.

Practice Example

Imagine someone says, "You're only defending this new school policy because you're a teacher and it helps you." This is the *Appeal to Motive* Fallacy because it attacks the person's possible interest in the policy rather than addressing its pros and cons. A more rational approach would be to discuss the actual benefits or drawbacks of the policy itself.

Defending Against the *Appeal to Motive* Fallacy

When someone dismisses an argument based on motives, here's how to bring the focus back to the content:

- **Ask for Evidence Supporting or Disproving the Argument**

  Say, "Let's look at the argument itself—what evidence supports or opposes it?"

- **Point Out That Motivation Doesn't Change Facts**

  Gently add, "Even if they have a motive, it doesn't mean the argument is wrong."

- **Encourage Evaluating the Argument Separately**

  Suggest, "Let's consider the points being made, regardless of possible motives."

By recognizing the Appeal to Motive Fallacy, you'll stay focused on the content of arguments and avoid dismissing ideas based on personal suspicions. But sometimes, chance events are mistakenly seen as meaningful connections. Let's unpack this fallacy!

Chapter 67: The Appeal to Coincidence Fallacy

The *Appeal to Coincidence* Fallacy happens when someone explains away a pattern or connection as mere coincidence, despite strong evidence suggesting a cause. It's like saying, "It's just a coincidence that sales always increase when we advertise," even if the data consistently shows a clear link between advertising and higher sales. Here, the argument relies on attributing outcomes to chance, even when there's likely a cause at play.

Why Is the *Appeal to Coincidence* a Fallacy?

The *Appeal to Coincidence* is flawed because it ignores the possibility of connection, even when there's substantial evidence of a link. Dismissing meaningful patterns or connections as "just coincidence" can prevent us from understanding the true cause of events. Sound reasoning means exploring possible causes rather than assuming outcomes are random.

Why Do Humans Use the *Appeal to Coincidence*?

Humans often use this fallacy because admitting a connection can be uncomfortable or challenging, especially if it means changing beliefs or behaviors. Attributing something to coincidence can feel easier than looking for real reasons or explanations. Recognizing this tendency helps us stay curious about possible causes and avoid shrugging off meaningful patterns.

How to Avoid the *Appeal to Coincidence* Fallacy

1. Look for Consistent Patterns

Ask yourself, "Is there a regular pattern that suggests a cause, or is this truly random?"

2. Examine Evidence for Causation

If there's data or research pointing to a link, consider it seriously rather than dismissing it as chance.

3. Stay Open to Causes, Even If They're Surprising

Be willing to explore unexpected explanations instead of labeling outcomes as coincidental.

Practice Example

Imagine someone says, "It's just a coincidence that I always feel better after drinking more water." If they consistently feel better when hydrated, this might be a sign of causation rather than pure coincidence. A more rational approach would involve exploring whether increased hydration is genuinely helping.

Defending Against the *Appeal to Coincidence* Fallacy

When someone attributes a clear pattern to coincidence, here's how to bring the focus back to possible causes:

- **Ask About Potential Explanations**

  Say, "Could there be a reason this keeps happening instead of it being random?"

- **Point Out the Pattern**

  Suggest, "It's happening regularly, so maybe there's a connection worth exploring."

- **Encourage Examining the Evidence**

  Remind them, "If there's a consistent pattern, there might be a cause behind it."

By recognizing the *Appeal to Coincidence* Fallacy, you'll stay open to finding meaningful causes behind patterns, rather than dismissing them as chance. But there's another pitfall to watch for that involves twisting someone's words by taking them out of context. Let's explore this next fallacy.

Chapter 68: The Contextomy Fallacy

The *Contextomy* Fallacy occurs when someone takes a quote or statement out of its original context to change its meaning or make it support a different idea. It's like quoting a book review that says, "This film was amazing ... at making me want to leave the theater," but only using "This film was amazing." Here, the argument misrepresents the original statement to make it appear as if it supports an unrelated claim.

Why Is *Contextomy* a Fallacy?

The *Contextomy* Fallacy is flawed because it misleads by manipulating language. Taking words out of context can completely change their meaning, often to favor one perspective unfairly. Sound reasoning requires quoting accurately and maintaining the original intent of statements. Misrepresentation prevents a fair and honest discussion.

Why Do Humans Use the *Contextomy* Fallacy?

Humans often use this fallacy because partial quotes can seem more powerful or persuasive, especially if they support an argument's goal. It's tempting to use someone's words against them by reshaping their meaning, but this approach isn't ethical or logical. Recognizing this tendency helps us stay honest in our discussions and avoid being misled by selective quoting.

How to Avoid the *Contextomy* Fallacy

1. Quote with Integrity

Ask yourself, "Am I preserving the original meaning of this quote?"

2. Provide Full Context

When using quotes, include enough context so readers or listeners understand the original intent.

3. Read the Surrounding Text

Make sure you understand the full message or argument before using a quote to support a claim.

Practice Example

Imagine someone says, "The author of this article thinks this policy is great!" by quoting, "This policy is great … at creating more problems." Here, the quote is taken out of context to change its meaning. A more honest approach would include the full statement, showing that the author was actually criticizing the policy.

Defending Against the *Contextomy* Fallacy

When someone uses an out-of-context quote to support their argument, here's how to encourage a return to the full meaning:

• Ask to See the Full Quote

Say, "Can we look at the original statement to see the full context?"

• Point Out Misinterpretations

Suggest, "This quote may have a different meaning in its full form. Let's check to be sure."

• Encourage Honest Representation

Remind them, "Using quotes accurately helps keep the discussion fair."

By recognizing the *Contextomy* Fallacy, you'll promote fair discussions that respect the true meaning of people's words. Excellent work—each fallacy you learn helps you interpret information honestly and accurately! But sometimes, vivid examples can create a powerful impression that outweighs the actual facts. Let's unpack this next fallacy.

Chapter 69: The Misleading Vividness Fallacy

The *Misleading Vividness* Fallacy happens when someone overestimates the probability of an event happening because of one powerful or memorable example, rather than looking at broader data. It's like saying, "My friend got sick after flying, so flying is dangerous for your health!" Here, the argument relies on a single, vivid incident rather than statistics or evidence that reflect the actual risks.

Why Is *Misleading Vividness* a Fallacy?

The *Misleading Vividness* Fallacy is flawed because a single example doesn't represent the larger pattern or likelihood of something happening. Just because one memorable event occurred doesn't mean it's common. Rational thinking requires looking at the big picture, which is often less dramatic than isolated incidents might suggest.

Why Do Humans Use the *Misleading Vividness* Fallacy?

Humans often fall into this fallacy because vivid stories or examples create strong emotional impressions that feel more real than abstract statistics. Our minds are wired to remember and react to dramatic events, but this can lead us to misjudge how often those events happen. Recognizing this tendency helps us make decisions based on actual probabilities, rather than memorable anecdotes.

How to Avoid the *Misleading Vividness* Fallacy

1. Consider the Full Picture

Ask yourself, "Does this example represent the broader data, or is it just an isolated incident?"

2. Seek Statistical Evidence

Look at the actual statistics or probability of an event rather than relying on a single story.

3. Acknowledge That Emotional Impact Doesn't Equal Frequency

Just because an event feels memorable doesn't mean it happens often.

Practice Example

Imagine someone says, "I heard about someone who won the lottery twice, so it must be possible to win big more than once." While it's possible, it's also extremely rare, and this example doesn't reflect the true odds. A more logical approach would be to look at the probability of winning the lottery even once, let alone twice.

Defending Against the *Misleading Vividness* Fallacy

When someone uses a single vivid example to generalize, here's how to encourage them to consider the broader picture:

- **Ask About Statistical Evidence**

  Say, "What do the numbers show about the overall likelihood of this happening?"

- **Point Out That Isolated Incidents Aren't the Norm**

  Suggest, "A single case doesn't make something common. Let's look at the bigger picture."

- **Remind Them That Dramatic Examples Can Skew Perception**

  Gently add, "Sometimes dramatic stories stick with us, but they don't always reflect the true odds."

By recognizing the *Misleading Vividness* Fallacy, you'll be able to make decisions based on reality rather than on isolated, memorable examples. But be careful — sometimes, arguments unfairly lean on claims of privilege to dismiss or deflect ideas. Let's explore this further.

Chapter 70: The Appeal to Privilege Fallacy

The *Appeal to Privilege* Fallacy occurs when someone dismisses another person's argument or concerns by claiming that they're "too privileged" to understand the issue. It's like saying, "You can't talk about healthcare because you're rich and don't get it." Here, the argument is dismissed based on the person's perceived privilege rather than on the merits of what they're actually saying.

Why Is the *Appeal to Privilege* a Fallacy?

The *Appeal to Privilege* is flawed because a person's background doesn't necessarily affect the validity of their arguments. Just because someone may not have directly experienced an issue doesn't mean their perspective or evidence is automatically invalid. Good reasoning requires engaging with the argument itself, rather than assuming someone's background makes their point irrelevant.

Why Do Humans Use the *Appeal to Privilege*?

Humans use this fallacy because it can be tempting to assume that those who haven't experienced an issue firsthand can't understand it or contribute valuable perspectives. Sometimes, privilege can limit understanding, but this assumption alone isn't enough to reject someone's argument. Recognizing this fallacy helps us evaluate claims on their logic and evidence, not on who is making them.

How to Avoid the *Appeal to Privilege*

1. Focus on the Argument's Validity

Ask yourself, "Does the argument make sense, regardless of the person's background?"

2. Acknowledge Perspective Without Dismissing Insight

Recognize that while someone's background may affect their viewpoint, it doesn't invalidate the reasoning.

3. Separate the Person from the Point

Evaluate the argument independently of the person's privilege or experience level.

Practice Example

Imagine someone says, "Public education funding should be a top priority." The response, "You went to private school, so you don't understand public education issues," is an example of the *Appeal to Privilege* Fallacy. A more constructive response would engage with the person's point about education funding, regardless of their personal experience.

Defending Against the *Appeal to Privilege* Fallacy

When someone dismisses an argument based on privilege, here's how to keep the focus on the message:

- **Ask About the Argument's Content**

  Say, "Is there anything incorrect in the argument itself?"

- **Point Out That Ideas Stand Alone**

  Remind them, "An argument's value isn't dependent on the person's background."

- **Encourage Evaluating the Point, Not the Person**

  Suggest, "Let's focus on the argument itself to see if it holds up."

By recognizing the *Appeal to Privilege* Fallacy, you'll focus on evaluating arguments based on their logic, not on assumptions about the person presenting them. But sometimes, the mere possibility of something happening is mistaken for certainty. Let's explore this next fallacy!

Chapter 71: The Appeal to Equivocation Fallacy

The *Appeal to Possibility* Fallacy happens when someone assumes that because something *could* happen, it *will* happen, or that it's highly probable. It's like saying, "There's a chance I could win the lottery, so I'll start planning what I'll buy!" Here, the argument confuses what's possible with what's probable, even if the likelihood of the event is extremely low.

Why Is the *Appeal to Possibility* a Fallacy?

The *Appeal to Possibility* is flawed because the fact that something *can* happen doesn't mean it will happen. Rational thinking means distinguishing between what's theoretically possible and what's realistically probable. Without evidence indicating that something is likely, assuming it will happen is misleading.

Why Do Humans Use the *Appeal to Possibility*?

Humans often fall into this fallacy because it's exciting or reassuring to focus on potential outcomes, even if they're unlikely. The idea that "anything is possible" is tempting, but without evidence, it can lead to unrealistic assumptions. Recognizing this tendency helps us make more balanced decisions based on what's actually likely, not just what's conceivable.

How to Avoid the *Appeal to Possibility*

1. Ask About the Likelihood

Ask yourself, "Is there evidence that this will likely happen, or is it just a possibility?"

2. Focus on Probability, Not Just Possibility

Consider whether there are real reasons to expect an outcome, beyond just the fact that it could theoretically occur.

3. Recognize the Difference Between Possible and Probable

Stay grounded in the data or evidence that indicates likelihood, not just feasibility.

Practice Example

Imagine someone says, "I might become famous one day, so I should start preparing for fame now!" While it's possible to become famous, it's not probable for most people. A more balanced approach would consider the steps that could make fame more probable and focus on realistic goals.

Defending Against the *Appeal to Possibility* Fallacy

When someone assumes that something will happen just because it's possible, here's how to help them think in terms of probability:

- **Ask About Evidence for Probability**

  Say, "Is there any evidence that this is likely, or just that it's possible?"

- **Encourage Thinking About Realistic Outcomes**

  Suggest, "Let's consider how probable this outcome is compared to other scenarios."

- **Point Out That Possibility Doesn't Guarantee Probability**

  Gently remind them, "Just because it can happen doesn't mean it will."

By recognizing the *Appeal to Possibility* Fallacy, you'll make more realistic decisions based on what's likely, not just what's conceivable. Great work—each fallacy you learn strengthens your ability to make sound judgments and stay grounded in reality! But there's another trap to watch for — one that exaggerates disagreements to make issues seem more polarized than they are. Let's take a look at this next fallacy!

Chapter 72: The Inflation of Conflict Fallacy

The *Inflation of Conflict* Fallacy occurs when someone assumes that if experts disagree on a topic, it must mean that all opinions are equally valid or that the truth lies somewhere in between. It's like saying, "Since scientists don't all agree on climate change, it's probably not that big of a deal." Here, the argument relies on the idea that any level of disagreement between experts creates enough doubt to invalidate one or both sides.

Why Is the *Inflation of Conflict* a Fallacy?

The *Inflation of Conflict* is flawed because it exaggerates disagreements, often ignoring the weight of evidence that supports one side more than the other. Just because a small number of experts disagree doesn't mean the entire topic is uncertain or that the truth lies in the middle. Rational thinking requires looking at the overall evidence, consensus, and credibility of sources, not just the presence of any disagreement.

Why Do Humans Use the Inflation of Conflict?

Humans often use this fallacy because disagreements among experts can make a topic feel confusing or unreliable. By assuming both sides are equally valid or that the truth must lie in between, they avoid the effort of examining the actual evidence. Recognizing this tendency helps us understand that not all conflicts are equally balanced, and some positions may be far better supported than others.

How to Avoid the *Inflation of Conflict* Fallacy

1. Consider the Weight of Evidence

Ask yourself, "What does the majority of credible evidence show, rather than focusing on outliers?"

2. Recognize That Not All Opinions Are Equal

Just because an opinion exists doesn't mean it has as much merit as a well-supported view.

3. Evaluate Expertise and Consensus

Look at the level of agreement among qualified experts and the strength of the evidence, rather than just noting the existence of disagreement.

Practice Example

Imagine someone says, "Since some doctors don't agree about the effectiveness of vaccines, the science must be uncertain." This is the Inflation of Conflict Fallacy because it implies that a small amount of disagreement nullifies the overwhelming evidence supporting vaccines. A more logical approach would be to look at the large consensus of research rather than focusing on the minority who disagree.

Defending Against the *Inflation of Conflict* Fallacy

When someone assumes that expert disagreement means a topic is completely unsettled, here's how to encourage them to look at the overall evidence:

- **Point to the Consensus Among Experts**

  Say, "Most qualified experts agree on this, even if a few disagree."

- **Ask About the Quality of Evidence**

  Suggest, "Let's look at the strength of the evidence rather than focusing on isolated opinions."

- **Remind Them That Disagreement Doesn't Mean Equal Validity**

  Gently add, "Just because there's some disagreement doesn't mean all views are equally supported."

By recognizing the *Inflation of Conflict* Fallacy, you'll be able to make decisions based on well-supported evidence rather than assuming all conflicts are balanced. However, arguments sometimes invoke complex science to make ideas sound credible without proper context. Let's dive into this next fallacy!

Chapter 73: The Appeal to Quantum Physics Fallacy

The *Appeal to Quantum* Physics Fallacy happens when someone uses complex scientific terms, often from quantum physics or other advanced fields, to make a claim sound credible, even if it has little to do with the actual science. It's like saying, "Quantum physics shows that everything is connected, so positive thinking will change reality." Here, the argument relies on the perceived mystery and authority of quantum science to give an unrelated idea credibility.

Why Is the *Appeal to Quantum Physics* a Fallacy?

The *Appeal to Quantum Physics* is flawed because it misuses scientific terms and concepts to support ideas without real evidence or understanding. Quantum physics is complex, but this doesn't mean it can be applied randomly to unrelated topics. Sound reasoning requires that concepts are used accurately, with clear explanations of how they're relevant to the argument being made.

Why Do Humans Use the *Appeal to Quantum Physics*?

Humans often use this fallacy because quantum physics is famously mysterious and complex, giving it an air of authority. For many, using such terms can make an argument seem deep or profound, even if the science isn't connected to the topic. Recognizing this fallacy helps us stay grounded in logic, separating genuine science from buzzwords and pseudoscience.

How to Avoid the *Appeal to Quantum Physics*

1. Ask for Clear Explanations

Ask yourself, "Does the person explain how this science actually applies, or are they just using it to sound impressive?"

2. Check for Relevance

Make sure the scientific concept is actually relevant to the argument instead of being thrown in without connection.

3. Be Cautious of Complex Jargon in Non-Scientific Topics

If scientific language is used without explanation, consider whether it's really necessary or just an attempt to add authority.

Practice Example

Imagine someone says, "Quantum mechanics proves that our thoughts can directly shape reality." This is *the Appeal to Quantum Physics* Fallacy because it uses quantum mechanics, a complex field of science, to make a claim without scientific backing or evidence connecting the two. A more logical approach would be to ask for clear, credible research linking quantum mechanics with human thought, rather than assuming such a connection.

Defending Against the *Appeal to Quantum Physics* Fallacy

When someone uses complex scientific terms to make an unrelated claim, here's how to bring the discussion back to clarity:

- **Ask for a Clear Connection**

  Say, "Can you explain how quantum physics directly relates to this idea?"

- **Encourage Looking for Real Evidence**

  Suggest, "Let's see if there's credible research supporting this connection, rather than relying on mystery."

- **Point Out the Difference Between Science and Buzzwords**

  Gently add, "Sometimes, science terms are used to make things sound impressive, but they may not apply here."

By recognizing the *Appeal to Quantum Physics* Fallacy, you'll focus on clear reasoning rather than being distracted by scientific buzzwords that may not actually apply. But there's another bias to watch out for — the tendency to assume that everyone shares your beliefs or opinions. Let's unpack this next fallacy.

Chapter 74: The False Consensus Effect

The *False Consensus Effect* happens when someone assumes that most people think or feel the same way they do, even if there's little evidence to support it. It's like saying, "Everyone probably agrees that pineapple on pizza is terrible," just because that's what *you* believe.

Why Is the *False Consensus Effect* a Fallacy?

The *False Consensus Effect* is flawed because it leads to biased thinking, where one's own beliefs are seen as universal truths. Just because something feels right or obvious doesn't mean it's a widely held opinion. Rational thinking means recognizing that others may have different experiences, values, or preferences, and that our own views are not automatically universal.

Why Do Humans Use the *False Consensus Effect*?

Humans often fall into this fallacy because it's comforting to assume that our beliefs are shared, making us feel validated and supported. We're also naturally biased toward our own perspectives, making it easy to project our views onto others. Recognizing this tendency helps us stay open to different perspectives and avoid making assumptions about what "everyone" thinks.

How to Avoid the *False Consensus Effect*

1. Acknowledge Diverse Perspectives

Ask yourself, "What are other viewpoints people might have on this issue?"

2. Seek Evidence of Broader Opinion

Rather than assuming, look for actual data or surveys to understand what others believe.

3. Stay Curious About Other Views

Accept that people may have different experiences, which shape their beliefs and preferences.

Practice Example

Imagine someone says, "No one enjoys reading instruction manuals; they're boring for everyone." This is an example of the *False Consensus Effect*, as it assumes a personal dislike is universally shared. A more balanced approach would be to recognize that some people may actually enjoy manuals, especially if they find them useful or interesting.

Defending Against the *False Consensus Effect*

When someone assumes that "everyone" shares their view, here's how to encourage them to consider other perspectives:

- **Ask About the Basis for Their Belief**

  Say, "Do we know if most people feel this way, or could it just be a personal preference?"

- **Encourage Considering Other Viewpoints**

  Suggest, "It's possible that others have different views based on their experiences."

- **Point Out the Value of Diverse Opinions**

  Remind them, "People see things differently, which can be helpful to consider."

By recognizing the *False Consensus Effect*, you'll be open to understanding others' views and avoid the trap of assuming everyone thinks like you. But there's another trap to watch out for — one that attempts to sway opinions by appealing to bitterness or resentment. Let's investigate this next fallacy!

Chapter 75: The Appeal to Spite Fallacy

The *Appeal to Spite* Fallacy happens when someone tries to win an argument by stirring up feelings of bitterness, resentment, or spite toward an opposing idea or person. It's like saying, "Why should we support that charity? Remember how rude they were to us last year?" Here, the argument relies on provoking negative emotions to distract from the actual issue, rather than presenting logical reasons.

Why Is the *Appeal to Spite* a Fallacy?

The *Appeal to Spite* is flawed because emotions like bitterness or resentment don't provide evidence about the validity of an idea. When arguments are based on anger or grudges, they're often trying to bypass logic and encourage a knee-jerk reaction instead. Rational thinking means evaluating the issue itself, not letting past resentments cloud judgment.

Why Do Humans Use the *Appeal to Spite*?

Humans often fall into this fallacy because feelings of spite or resentment can be powerful and persuasive, especially if they have a personal history or a bad experience. It's easy to let negative emotions take over in arguments, but this can lead to decisions based on anger rather than evidence. Recognizing this tendency helps us approach issues fairly, focusing on the facts rather than personal grievances.

How to Avoid the *Appeal to Spite*

1. Separate Emotion from Evidence

Ask yourself, "Am I being swayed by negative emotions, or is there a logical reason to believe this?"

2. Focus on the Current Issue

Avoid bringing up unrelated past grievances when evaluating an argument.

3. Stay Open to Ideas Despite Negative Feelings

Recognize that emotions like bitterness may not be relevant to the truth of the matter.

Practice Example

Imagine someone says, "Don't vote for that candidate—they come from the same school as that rude teacher we had." This is an *Appeal to Spite* Fallacy, as it tries to draw on resentment toward an unrelated person to sway an opinion about the candidate. A more logical approach would focus on the candidate's policies, not personal bitterness.

Defending Against the *Appeal to Spite* Fallacy

When someone uses bitterness or resentment to try to persuade you, here's how to keep the focus on the actual issue:

- **Ask About the Facts**

  Say, "What does this have to do with the actual point we're discussing?"

- **Encourage Setting Aside Personal Grudges**

  Suggest, "Let's evaluate this idea on its own merits, without bringing past issues into it."

- **Remind Them That Spite Doesn't Equal Reason**

  Gently add, "Bitterness doesn't make an argument stronger—it just makes it emotional."

By recognizing the *Appeal to Spite* Fallacy, you'll stay grounded in fair, evidence-based reasoning rather than letting past grudges influence your judgments. But sometimes, people accept ideas as true simply because they feel personally meaningful. Let's explore this next fallacy!

Chapter 76: The Subjective Validation Fallacy

The *Subjective Validation* Fallacy happens when someone accepts an idea or claim as true because it feels personally meaningful or resonates with them, rather than because of solid evidence. It's like saying, "This horoscope feels so accurate—it must be true!" Here, the argument relies on the personal relevance of a statement, rather than any objective support for its truth.

Why Is *Subjective Validation* a Fallacy?

The *Subjective Validation* Fallacy is flawed because personal feelings and beliefs don't determine truth. While it's natural to feel more connected to ideas that reflect our personal experiences, this doesn't make those ideas factually accurate. Rational thinking requires looking beyond personal resonance and seeking external, verifiable evidence to determine whether a claim is valid.

Why Do Humans Use *Subjective Validation*?

Humans often fall into this fallacy because we're naturally drawn to ideas that feel relevant or meaningful to us. Personal experiences shape how we see the world, and we may be inclined to accept information that reflects our own lives, memories, or values. Recognizing this tendency helps us stay objective and avoid mistaking personal relevance for universal truth.

How to Avoid *Subjective Validation*

1. Look for External Evidence

Ask yourself, "Is there objective evidence supporting this idea, or am I relying on how it feels to me?"

2. Distinguish Between Meaningful and True

Recognize that an idea can feel meaningful without necessarily being factual.

3. Seek Broader Perspectives

Consider whether the idea holds up under scrutiny from others who don't share the same personal context.

Practice Example

Imagine someone says, "I read my horoscope today, and it feels so accurate, so astrology must be real." This is an example of Subjective Validation because the person is accepting astrology as true based on how personally meaningful the horoscope feels, rather than on evidence that astrology can predict outcomes. A more logical approach would involve looking for reliable data or studies on astrology's accuracy.

Defending Against the *Subjective Validation* Fallacy

When someone accepts a belief because it feels personally meaningful, here's how to bring the focus back to objective evaluation:

- **Ask About the Evidence**

  Say, "What evidence supports this beyond it feeling personally relevant?"

- **Encourage Separating Feeling from Fact**

  Suggest, "Just because something feels right doesn't mean it's necessarily true."

- **Remind Them That Meaning and Truth Aren't Always the Same**

  Gently add, "It's okay for something to feel meaningful, but truth often requires more than personal validation."

By recognizing the *Subjective Validation* Fallacy, you can stay focused on objective evidence, avoiding the trap of mistaking personal meaning for universal truth. Excellent work — each fallacy you learn sharpens your critical thinking and keeps you rooted in reality! But there's another pitfall to watch out for — seeing connections between events that are actually unrelated. Let's explore this next fallacy!

Chapter 77: The Parataxic Reasoning Fallacy

The *Parataxic Reasoning* Fallacy happens when someone assumes that two unrelated events are causally connected, even if there's no real link between them. This fallacy often leads to superstitious thinking, like saying, "I wore my lucky socks, and we won the game, so the socks caused the win!" Here, the argument is based on an imagined causal link between events that just happened to coincide.

Why Is *Parataxic Reasoning* a Fallacy?

Parataxic Reasoning is flawed because it confuses correlation with causation, leading to conclusions that have no factual basis. Just because two events happen around the same time doesn't mean one caused the other. Rational thinking requires investigating whether a real causal connection exists rather than assuming one based on coincidence or patterns.

Why Do Humans Use *Parataxic Reasoning*?

Humans often fall into this fallacy because we're naturally inclined to look for patterns and meaning in events, even when they're random. This tendency has deep roots in human psychology, helping us make sense of the world, but it can lead to superstitions and incorrect assumptions about cause and effect. Recognizing this fallacy helps us remain skeptical of coincidences and seek logical explanations.

How to Avoid *Parataxic Reasoning*

1. Look for Evidence of a Real Link

Ask yourself, "Is there actual evidence showing that one event caused the other?"

2. Distinguish Between Coincidence and Cause

Remember that just because two things happen together doesn't mean they're connected.

3. Stay Skeptical of Patterns Without Proof

Avoid drawing conclusions based on coincidences or gut feelings about connections.

Practice Example

Imagine someone says, "Every time I carry my lucky coin, I have a good day, so the coin must be bringing me luck." This is an example of *Parataxic Reasoning*, as the person is attributing good days to the coin without any evidence of a real causal link. A more logical approach would be to recognize that positive and negative experiences can happen randomly, with no connection to the coin.

Defending Against the *Parataxic Reasoning* Fallacy

When someone assumes a cause-and-effect relationship based on coincidence, here's how to help them consider other explanations:

- **Ask for Evidence of Causation**

  Say, "What makes you think these events are connected rather than just coincidental?"

- **Encourage Skepticism Toward Coincidences**

  Suggest, "Coincidences happen all the time. It's worth considering whether this is just a pattern."

- **Remind Them That Patterns Don't Always Imply Cause**

  Gently add, "Seeing a pattern doesn't necessarily mean there's a cause behind it."

By recognizing the *Parataxic Reasoning* Fallacy, you'll avoid making assumptions about cause and effect based solely on coincidences or superstitions. But even when a flaw is found in an argument, it doesn't always mean the conclusion is false. Let's discuss this next fallacy.

Chapter 78: The Argument from Fallacy (Fallacist's Fallacy)

The *Argument from Fallacy*, or Fallacist's Fallacy, happens when someone assumes that because an argument contains a fallacy, its conclusion must be false. It's like saying, "You used a slippery slope argument to support recycling, so recycling must not be beneficial." Here, the person assumes that any error in reasoning automatically invalidates the conclusion, even though the conclusion might still be correct for other reasons.

Why Is This a Fallacy?

The *Argument from Fallacy* is flawed because just as a valid argument doesn't always lead to a true conclusion, a flawed argument doesn't necessarily lead to a false one. A conclusion can be true or false regardless of how it's argued. Rational thinking requires evaluating the conclusion independently, rather than assuming it's false just because it was poorly supported.

Why Do Humans Use the *Argument from Fallacy*?

Humans often fall into this fallacy because spotting a flaw in someone's argument can feel like a "gotcha" moment, leading to an assumption that the entire conclusion must be incorrect. This mistake is often a natural reaction to seeing errors in reasoning, but it overlooks the possibility that the conclusion might still be valid on its own merits. Recognizing this fallacy helps them keep an open mind and judge conclusions based on evidence rather than the way they're argued.

How to Avoid the *Argument from Fallacy*

1. Evaluate the Conclusion Separately

Ask yourself, "Does this conclusion stand up on its own, regardless of how it was argued?"

2. Consider Alternative Reasons for the Conclusion

Recognize that even if the argument is flawed, there may still be valid support for the conclusion.

3. Avoid Dismissing Conclusions Based on Argument Quality Alone

Understand that an argument's flaws don't guarantee that the conclusion is wrong.

Practice Example

Imagine someone says, "Eating vegetables is healthy because my grandmother says so." You might spot the *Appeal to Authority Fallacy* here, but this doesn't mean that eating vegetables is unhealthy. The conclusion might still be true, even though the argument used to support it is weak. A more logical approach would be to evaluate whether other evidence supports the health benefits of vegetables.

Defending Against the *Argument from Fallacy*

When someone dismisses a conclusion solely because of a fallacy in the argument, here's how to help them consider the conclusion independently:

- **Ask Them to Evaluate the Conclusion Directly**

  Say, "Even if the argument was flawed, is there still reason to believe the conclusion?"

- **Encourage Separating Argument Quality from Truth**

  Suggest, "Let's look at the conclusion separately to see if it might still be valid."

- **Point Out That Bad Arguments Can Support True Conclusions**

  Gently add, "Just because the argument is flawed doesn't mean the conclusion has to be wrong."

By recognizing the *Argument from Fallacy*, you'll avoid dismissing ideas solely because of flawed arguments and stay open to conclusions that may be correct for other reasons. But sometimes, patterns can emerge that aren't really there, leading to conclusions based on imagined connections, as we discuss in our next fallacy.

Chapter 78: The Apophenia Fallacy

The *Apophenia* Fallacy happens when someone perceives meaningful patterns or connections in random data, even when there's no real relationship between the pieces of information. It's like saying, "Every time I see a black cat, something bad happens, so the cat must be causing bad luck."

Why Is *Apophenia* a Fallacy?

Apophenia is flawed because it assigns meaning or causation to random events, leading to incorrect conclusions. Humans are naturally inclined to search for patterns, but just because events seem connected doesn't mean they are. Rational thinking requires questioning whether patterns are meaningful or if they might just be coincidences in random data.

Why Do Humans Use Apophenia?

Humans often fall into this fallacy because their brains are wired to recognize patterns, which helped early humans make sense of their surroundings. However, this tendency can backfire, leading them to see connections where none exist, fueling superstitions and even conspiracy theories. Recognizing apophenia helps them stay grounded in reality, seeking evidence before concluding that events are connected.

How to Avoid *Apophenia*

1. Question the Connection

Ask yourself, "Is there any evidence that these events are actually related?"

2. Look for Alternative Explanations

Recognize that many patterns are coincidences rather than signs of cause and effect.

3. Seek Evidence, Not Intuition

Avoid relying on gut feelings alone and look for concrete proof of any supposed link.

Practice Example

Imagine someone says, "Every time there's a full moon, I notice more strange things happening around town. The moon must be affecting people's behavior." This is an example of apophenia, as it assumes a meaningful connection based on coincidence. A more logical approach would be to look for studies examining whether the full moon genuinely impacts human behavior, rather than relying on observations alone.

Defending Against the *Apophenia* Fallacy

When someone sees a pattern in random events, here's how to help them consider whether there's truly a connection:

- **Ask for Evidence of a Real Link**

  Say, "Is there any proof showing these events are actually connected?"

- **Encourage Thinking About Coincidences**

  Suggest, "Sometimes things just happen to coincide without being connected."

- **Point Out the Difference Between Pattern and Proof**

  Gently add, "Seeing a pattern doesn't mean there's a real cause behind it. Evidence is what proves a link."

By recognizing the *Apophenia* Fallacy, you'll be cautious of seeing patterns in randomness and avoid jumping to conclusions without solid evidence. Each fallacy you learn helps you think critically and spot the difference between coincidence and causation. But there's another subtle trap to watch for — confusing what's essential with what's enough. Let's explore this next fallacy!

Chapter 80: Confusing Necessary and Sufficient Conditions

The fallacy of *Confusing Necessary and Sufficient Conditions* happens when someone mistakenly assumes that a necessary condition for something is also sufficient to achieve it, or vice versa. It's like saying, "Having flour is enough to make a cake," even though you need more ingredients. Here, the argument is flawed because it doesn't recognize the difference between conditions that are *required* versus those that are *enough*.

Why Is *Confusing Necessary and Sufficient Conditions* a Fallacy?

This fallacy is flawed because it mixes up two types of conditions:

- A **necessary condition** is something that must be true for an outcome to happen, but it's not always enough on its own.

- A **sufficient condition** is enough to produce the outcome but isn't always required.
- Rational thinking requires distinguishing between what's *required* for an outcome and what's *enough* to bring it about.

Why Do Humans Confuse *Necessary and Sufficient Conditions*?

Humans often fall into this fallacy because it can be tricky to tell the difference between what's needed and what's enough. They're used to thinking in simple cause-and-effect terms, which can blur these distinctions. Recognizing this fallacy helps them clarify whether something is merely part of a bigger solution or if it's the whole answer.

How to Avoid *Confusing Necessary and Sufficient Conditions*

1. Ask Whether Each Condition Alone Is Enough

Determine whether a condition just helps or if it's truly sufficient to cause an outcome.

2. Separate Requirements from Solutions

Identify conditions that are merely needed versus those that fully solve the problem.

3. Check for Additional Requirements

Consider what other factors might be necessary to achieve the outcome.

Practice Example

Imagine someone says, "If you want to be successful, you just need to work hard." This confuses a necessary condition with a sufficient one, since hard work alone doesn't guarantee success. A more accurate approach would recognize that while hard work is important, other factors (like resources and opportunities) might also be required.

Defending Against This Fallacy

When someone confuses necessary and sufficient conditions, here's how to help clarify their reasoning:

- **Ask if the Condition Is Enough on Its Own**

  Say, "Is this condition sufficient by itself, or is it just one part of what's needed?"

- **Encourage Identifying All Conditions**

  Suggest, "Let's look at other factors that might also be necessary."

- **Point Out the Difference Between Helping and Solving**

  Gently add, "This may be necessary, but it doesn't mean it's enough on its own."

By recognizing the difference between necessary and sufficient conditions, you'll be able to understand complex issues with clarity and precision. But be careful—sometimes arguments shift meaning by using biased definitions to make a point seem stronger. Let's discuss this next fallacy.

Chapter 81: The Definist Fallacy

The *Definist* Fallacy happens when someone uses biased or loaded definitions to support their argument, rather than providing objective evidence. It's like saying, "Only truly intelligent people like chess," where "intelligent" is defined to imply a preference for chess. Here, the argument is based on a definition crafted to favor the speaker's view, rather than a fair or neutral perspective.

Why Is This a Fallacy?

The *Definist* Fallacy is flawed because it uses biased definitions to make an argument seem true without addressing the issue itself. By incorporating an opinion into the definition, it sidesteps rational debate, making it seem as if only one answer is possible. Sound reasoning requires using fair, objective definitions that don't preemptively support one side of the argument.

Why Do Humans Use the *Definist* Fallacy?

Humans often fall into this fallacy because it can be persuasive to redefine terms in a way that supports their view. By controlling the language, they can sway the conversation to make it harder for others to disagree. Recognizing this tendency helps them spot attempts to redefine terms to suit an agenda, keeping discussions fair and objective.

How to Avoid the *Definist* Fallacy

1. Use Objective, Agreed-Upon Definitions

Ask yourself, "Is this definition neutral, or does it seem crafted to favor one side?"

2. Avoid Definitions That Imply a Conclusion

Make sure your definitions describe rather than imply a judgment.

3. Encourage Consistency in Terminology

Use the same definition consistently, rather than adjusting it to fit your view.

Practice Example

Imagine someone says, "Real patriots support every decision their country makes." This is an example of the *Definist* Fallacy, as it defines "patriot" in a biased way that excludes anyone who might question government decisions. A more objective approach would define patriotism as a love of country, which can include both support and constructive criticism.

Defending Against the *Definist* Fallacy

When someone uses a biased definition to make an argument, here's how to bring the focus back to fair definitions:

• Ask for a Neutral Definition

Say, "Can we use a definition that doesn't imply a conclusion?"

- **Encourage Consistency in Language**

  Suggest, "Let's agree on a definition that allows for different views."

- **Point Out the Impact of Loaded Language**

  Gently add, "Using a biased definition can prevent a fair discussion of the issue."

By recognizing the *Definist* Fallacy, you'll keep discussions fair, ensuring that arguments are based on logic rather than cleverly biased definitions. Excellent work — each fallacy you learn helps you communicate with precision and integrity! But sometimes, arguments compare things that aren't really comparable, leading to flawed conclusions. Let's review this next fallacy!

Chapter 82: The False Analogy Fallacy

The *False Analogy* Fallacy happens when someone makes a weak or misleading comparison between two things that aren't really similar, suggesting they are the same when they're not. It's like saying, "Schools are like factories, so students must follow strict rules like factory workers." Here, the argument relies on a superficial comparison that doesn't hold up under closer examination.

Why Is the *False Analogy* a Fallacy?

The *False Analogy* Fallacy is flawed because it equates two things based on minor similarities while ignoring the important differences between them. Just because two things share certain characteristics doesn't mean they are truly comparable in other respects. Sound reasoning requires using analogies that reflect meaningful similarities, not just convenient ones.

Why Do Humans Use the *False Analogy* Fallacy?

Humans often fall into this fallacy because analogies can simplify complex issues, making arguments easier to understand or seem more relatable. However, oversimplifying with a weak analogy can lead to incorrect conclusions. Recognizing this tendency helps them assess whether an analogy actually clarifies or just confuses the argument.

How to Avoid the *False Analogy* Fallacy

1. Check the Strength of the Comparison

Ask yourself, "Do these things share essential characteristics, or are they only similar on the surface?"

2. Identify Important Differences

Make sure the analogy doesn't ignore critical distinctions between the two things.

3. Focus on Accurate, Relevant Comparisons

Use analogies that help explain without oversimplifying or misleading.

Practice Example

Imagine someone says, "Relying on medication to be healthy is like cheating on a test to get good grades." This is an example of the False Analogy Fallacy, as it compares two things that aren't truly comparable. Medication is a tool for managing health, whereas cheating is a dishonest shortcut. A more accurate analogy would focus on the unique role of medication in healthcare.

Defending Against the *False Analogy* Fallacy

When someone uses a weak or misleading analogy, here's how to help them reconsider the comparison:

• Ask About the Key Similarities

Say, "Are these things similar in ways that matter to this argument?"

• Encourage Focusing on Relevant Comparisons

Suggest, "Let's find an analogy that really fits this situation."

• Point Out the Limits of the Analogy

Gently add, "Analogies can help, but they need to capture the real essence of the situation."

By recognizing the *False Analogy* Fallacy, you'll focus on using accurate comparisons that truly clarify ideas, avoiding conclusions based on misleading analogies. But there's another trap to watch for — judging past actions by today's standards. Let's explore this next fallacy!

Chapter 83: The Anachronistic Fallacy

The *Anachronistic* Fallacy happens when someone evaluates historical figures, actions, or events by today's standards, rather than the norms or values of their own time. It's like saying, "This ancient ruler was unethical for not supporting democracy," even though democracy wasn't a concept in that society. Here, the argument imposes modern beliefs on a different historical context, leading to unfair or misleading judgments.

Why Is This a Fallacy?

The *Anachronistic* Fallacy is flawed because it ignores historical context, which is essential to understanding people and actions from the past. Just because we have different standards today doesn't mean those standards applied back then. Rational thinking requires evaluating people and events within their own context to gain a fair and accurate understanding.

Why Do Humans Use the *Anachronistic* Fallacy?

Humans often fall into this fallacy because it's easier to interpret the past using familiar, modern values. However, this can lead to oversimplified views of history and unfair criticism of past societies. Recognizing this tendency helps them understand the complexities of historical contexts and avoid projecting their beliefs backward.

How to Avoid the *Anachronistic* Fallacy

1. Research the Historical Context

Ask yourself, "What were the common beliefs, values, or norms during this time?"

2. Separate Modern Views from Historical Realities

Avoid assuming that past societies shared our current understanding of ethics or social structures.

3. Evaluate People by the Standards of Their Time

Consider whether an action was typical or acceptable in its historical setting, even if it seems wrong today.

Practice Example

Imagine someone says, "This historical figure was wrong for not supporting equal rights." While it's true that equal rights are important, the *Anachronistic* Fallacy assumes that this value was widely held in the past, which may not be accurate. A more balanced approach would look at whether this figure's actions were unusual or typical for their time.

Defending Against the *Anachronistic* Fallacy

When someone uses modern values to criticize the past, here's how to bring the focus back to historical context:

- **Ask About the Standards of the Time**

  Say, "What were the norms or beliefs in this society during that period?"

- **Encourage a Contextual Approach**

  Suggest, "Let's try to understand their actions based on the time they lived in."

- **Point Out the Importance of Context**

  Gently add, "Applying today's values to history can lead to misunderstandings."

By recognizing the *Anachronistic* Fallacy, you'll understand people and events within their historical settings, leading to a more accurate view of history. But sometimes, arguments shift subtly in response to challenges, making them hard to pin down. Let's discuss this next fallacy.

Chapter 84: The Hedging Fallacy

The *Hedging* Fallacy happens when someone changes or subtly modifies their argument in response to objections without actually addressing those objections. It's like saying, "Exercise is the best way to get healthy," then switching to, "Well, I meant exercise is *one* of the best ways," when challenged. Here, the argument shifts to avoid criticism instead of confronting it directly.

Why Is *Hedging* a Fallacy?

The *Hedging* Fallacy is flawed because it doesn't engage with counterarguments in a meaningful way. By subtly changing the argument's meaning, the speaker avoids answering objections, making it seem as if they've defended their point when they haven't. Rational thinking requires addressing objections directly rather than evading them by moving the goalposts.

Why Do Humans Use the *Hedging* Fallacy?

Humans often fall into this fallacy because they want to maintain their argument's validity while avoiding direct challenges. By slightly modifying the argument, it seems as if they're still correct without having to fully defend their point. Recognizing this tendency helps them hold ourselves and others accountable to the original statements made in discussions.

How to Avoid the *Hedging* Fallacy

1. Stick to Your Original Point

Ask yourself, "Am I changing my argument to avoid the challenge, or addressing it directly?"

2. Engage with Objections Honestly

Consider whether you can strengthen your argument without shifting its meaning.

3. Clarify or Correct If Needed

If you do need to modify your stance, be transparent about it rather than subtly changing definitions.

Practice Example

Imagine someone says, "This diet is guaranteed to work," but then, when faced with counterexamples, they say, "Well, it's one of the best diets for most people." This is an example of the Hedging Fallacy, as the speaker has adjusted their claim without addressing the original promise. A more logical approach would either defend or revise the original statement clearly.

Defending Against the *Hedging* Fallacy

When someone modifies their argument to dodge criticism, here's how to bring them back to their original point:

- **Ask for Consistency**

Say, "Can we stick with the original statement and discuss any concerns directly?"

- **Encourage Addressing the Objection**

Suggest, "It's best to tackle the objection without changing the argument."

- **Point Out the Change in the Argument**

Gently add, "It seems the argument has shifted— can we clarify what we're discussing?"

By recognizing the *Hedging* Fallacy, you can engage in clearer, more honest discussions that don't shift to avoid objections. But be cautious—sometimes, complex issues are oversimplified by blaming a single cause. Let's dive into this next fallacy!

Chapter 85: The Single Cause Fallacy

The *Single Cause* Fallacy happens when someone attributes an outcome to only one factor when, in reality, multiple factors are involved. It's like saying, "The company failed solely because of bad marketing," even though there may have been other issues, such as poor management or market competition. Here, the argument overlooks the complexity of most situations, leading to an oversimplified view.

Why Is *Single Cause* a Fallacy?

The *Single Cause* Fallacy is flawed because it ignores other contributing factors that might be equally or more significant. Many outcomes are the result of complex interactions between various causes, and reducing them to just one can lead to misunderstandings or unfair blame. Rational thinking requires considering all possible factors to understand the full picture.

Why Do Humans Use the *Single Cause* Fallacy?

Humans often fall into this fallacy because focusing on one factor makes complex situations easier to explain. However, this simplification can lead to biased judgments or incomplete understanding. Recognizing this tendency helps them appreciate the interconnected nature of causes and make more informed assessments.

How to Avoid the *Single Cause* Fallacy

1. Consider Multiple Factors

Ask yourself, "What other factors might have contributed to this outcome?"

2. Avoid Jumping to Simple Explanations

Recognize that complex situations rarely have just one cause.

3. Examine the Evidence for Each Factor

Look at how different causes might interact, rather than isolating one as the only explanation.

Practice Example

Imagine someone says, "The school's low test scores are only due to poor teaching." This is an example of the Single Cause Fallacy, as it overlooks other potential factors, like socioeconomic issues, resources, or student support. A more balanced approach would consider how multiple factors might influence test scores.

Defending Against the *Single Cause* Fallacy

When someone attributes an outcome to a single factor, here's how to help them consider other causes:

• Ask About Other Possible Influences

Say, "Could there be other factors involved in this outcome?"

- **Encourage a Broader Perspective**

  Suggest, "Let's look at the situation as a whole, considering all potential causes."

- **Point Out the Complexity of Situations**

  Gently add, "Most outcomes result from multiple factors, not just one."

By recognizing the *Single Cause* Fallacy, you'll stay aware of the complexity of causes and avoid oversimplifying outcomes. But sometimes, arguments lean on an idealized view of the past, assuming it was better simply because it's gone. Let's have a look at this next fallacy!

Chapter 86: The Argument from Nostalgia Fallacy

The *Argument from Nostalgia* Fallacy happens when someone argues that something is better simply because it's from the past. It's like saying, "Music from the '80s was the best because everything was better back then." Here, the argument relies on an idealized view of the past rather than on evidence of actual quality or improvement.

Why Is the *Argument from Nostalgia* a Fallacy?

The *Argument from Nostalgia* is flawed because it assumes that something from the past is inherently superior, which isn't always true. Just because something is old doesn't mean it's better, and time alone doesn't necessarily improve quality. Rational thinking requires looking at evidence of value or effectiveness, regardless of when something was made.

Why Do Humans Use the *Argument from Nostalgia*?

Humans often fall into this fallacy because the past can feel comforting, and memories may be idealized over time. Nostalgia also tends to emphasize positive memories while downplaying negative ones, creating a biased view of "the good old days." Recognizing this tendency helps them assess ideas or practices based on their actual value, rather than on fond memories alone.

How to Avoid the Argument from *Nostalgia*

1. Focus on Evidence of Value

Ask yourself, "Is this thing truly better, or do I just have fond memories of it?"

2. Separate Sentiment from Reality

Recognize that positive feelings about the past don't mean everything was actually better.

3. Evaluate Ideas on Their Own Merits

Look for current data or analysis rather than relying on tradition or familiarity alone.

Practice Example

Imagine someone says, "Technology has made everything worse. Life was simpler and better before the internet." This is an example of the Argument from Nostalgia, as it ignores the many positive aspects of modern technology. A more logical approach would weigh both the pros and cons of technological advances, rather than idealizing the past.

Defending Against the *Argument from Nostalgia* Fallacy

When someone argues that something was better just because it's from the past, here's how to bring the discussion back to the present:

- **Ask for Evidence of Improvement**

  Say, "Is there any evidence that the past version was actually better?"

- **Encourage Balancing Pros and Cons**

  Suggest, "Let's look at both the positives and negatives of the past and present."

- **Point Out That Time Alone Doesn't Equal Quality**

  Gently add, "Just because something's older doesn't mean it's better."

By recognizing the *Argument from Nostalgia* Fallacy, you'll avoid letting fond memories cloud your judgment and stay focused on evaluating ideas fairly. But beware — some arguments try to undermine trust before they even begin. Let's explore this next fallacy!

Chapter 87: Poisoning the Well

The *Poisoning the Well* Fallacy happens when someone presents negative information about a person or idea in advance to undermine their credibility before they even speak. It's like saying, "Don't listen to him—he always lies," right before he shares his opinion. Here, the argument relies on creating a bias against the person or position to sway others without addressing the actual content of their argument.

Why Is *Poisoning the Well* a Fallacy?

Poisoning the Well is flawed because it attempts to discredit someone without addressing their argument's merits. By presenting adverse information before someone speaks, it encourages people to dismiss them based on unrelated personal factors rather than on the validity of what they say. Rational thinking requires focusing on arguments themselves, not biased preconceptions set up to make us reject a speaker unfairly.

Why Do Humans Use *Poisoning the Well?*

Humans often use this fallacy because it's an easy way to sway opinions without having to engage with the other side's actual argument. By creating suspicion or bias before the person even speaks, the fallacy can prevent people from considering their points thoughtfully. Recognizing this tactic helps them approach ideas with fairness, avoiding unnecessary biases.

How to Avoid Poisoning the Well

1. Evaluate Arguments on Their Own

Ask yourself, "Am I focusing on the person or the actual argument?"

2. Avoid Relying on Preconceptions

Try to separate any prior information about a person from the validity of what they're currently saying.

3. Consider Each Statement Independently

Judge statements based on their content rather than on outside factors or past behaviors.

Practice Example

Imagine someone says, "Don't trust her opinion on environmental issues—she drives a big SUV." This is an example of Poisoning the Well, as it preemptively biases listeners against her view without considering the actual content of her opinion. A more fair approach would focus on the arguments she makes, regardless of her personal choices.

Defending Against the *Poisoning the Well* Fallacy

When someone tries to bias others by presenting adverse information beforehand, here's how to bring the focus back to the argument:

- **Ask About the Relevance of the Information**

  Say, "Is this information related to the point being discussed, or is it just about the person?"

- **Encourage Evaluating Arguments Directly**

  Suggest, "Let's consider what they're actually saying instead of focusing on this unrelated information."

- **Point Out the Need for Fairness**

  Gently add, "It's best to hear them out without any preconceptions that might cloud our judgment."

By recognizing *Poisoning the Well*, you'll approach discussions with a fair and open mind, judging ideas on their own merits. But sometimes, arguments use vague or slippery language to sound stronger than they are. Let's look at this this next fallacy.

Chapter 88: The Weasel Words Fallacy

The *Weasel Words* Fallacy happens when someone uses vague, non-committal language to make an argument sound stronger than it really is. It's like saying, "Many experts believe this diet could be the best option," without specifying who the experts are or how strong their belief is. Here, the argument relies on language that sounds impressive but avoids concrete details.

Why Are *Weasel Words* a Fallacy?

Weasel Words are a fallacy because they make a claim seem more convincing by adding ambiguity, making it difficult to assess the argument's real strength. By using terms that are open to interpretation, like "some say" or "it's widely believed," speakers can imply more support than actually exists. Rational thinking requires precise language that allows others to understand and evaluate the true claim being made.

Why Do Humans Use *Weasel Words*?

Humans often use Weasel Words to make arguments sound more credible without providing real evidence. Vague language allows speakers to dodge accountability for their claims, creating a false impression of strength or authority. Recognizing this tendency helps them look more closely at the actual support behind statements, rather than being swayed by ambiguous phrasing.

How to Avoid *Weasel Words*

1. Use Clear, Specific Language

Ask yourself, "Am I using language that directly states my claim, or am I being vague?"

2. Provide Sources and Examples

Back up claims with concrete information to avoid leaving them open to interpretation.

3. Avoid Generalized Statements Without Evidence

Refrain from using terms like "some say" or "many believe" without specifics to back them up.

Practice Example

Imagine someone says, "This product is known to provide excellent results." This is an example of the Weasel Words Fallacy because it uses vague terms like "known" and "excellent" without specifying who has found it effective or what those results are. A clearer statement would include specific studies, user reviews, or data that support the claim.

Defending Against the *Weasel Words* Fallacy

When someone uses vague language to make their point seem stronger, here's how to encourage clarity:

• Ask for Specifics

Say, "Who are the experts you mentioned? Could you provide specific examples?"

• Encourage Definite Language

Suggest, "It would help if we had more concrete information about who believes this and why."

• Point Out the Ambiguity

Gently add, "It's hard to evaluate this claim without clearer details about who and what is being referenced."

By recognizing *Weasel Words*, you'll seek out clear, specific language that makes arguments more honest and straightforward. But be careful — sometimes, arguments dismiss efforts as pointless if they can't solve a problem entirely. Let's explore this next fallacy!

Chapter 89: The Appeal to Futility Fallacy

The *Appeal to Futility* Fallacy happens when someone argues that an effort is pointless because it won't completely solve a problem or achieve a perfect outcome. It's like saying, "Recycling won't save the planet, so there's no use in doing it." Here, the argument suggests that because an action can't achieve 100% success, it's not worth attempting at all.

Why Is the *Appeal to Futility* a Fallacy?

The *Appeal to Futility* is flawed because progress and partial solutions can still make meaningful differences, even if they don't completely solve a problem. Just because an effort isn't perfect doesn't mean it's worthless. Rational thinking requires recognizing that small steps can contribute positively, even if they're not total solutions.

Why Do Humans Use the *Appeal to Futility*?

Humans often fall into this fallacy because it's easier to dismiss challenges than to make ongoing efforts. If perfection is the only acceptable outcome, anything less can feel insufficient, leading people to give up prematurely. Recognizing this tendency helps them stay motivated to make incremental improvements, even when they don't solve everything.

How to Avoid the *Appeal to Futility* Fallacy

1. Focus on Positive Impacts, Even if Partial

Ask yourself, "Does this effort make some improvement, even if it's not perfect?"

2. Recognize the Value of Small Contributions

Understand that many small steps can collectively lead to big changes over time.

3. Avoid All-or-Nothing Thinking

Embrace the idea that imperfect solutions can still help.

Practice Example

Imagine someone says, "Why bother voting? One vote won't change the outcome." This is an example of the *Appeal to Futility* Fallacy, as it ignores the cumulative impact of many individual votes. A more logical approach would recognize that each vote contributes to the overall outcome, even if one vote alone doesn't decide it.

Defending Against the *Appeal to Futility* Fallacy

When someone argues that an effort is pointless because it won't completely solve a problem, here's how to bring the focus back to incremental progress:

- **Ask About Partial Benefits**

Say, "Even if it doesn't solve everything, does it make a positive impact?"

- **Encourage Focusing on Collective Contributions**

Suggest, "Many small actions add up to make a difference."

- **Point Out the Value of Imperfect Solutions**

Gently add, "An imperfect solution is better than doing nothing."

By recognizing the *Appeal to Futility* Fallacy, you'll stay motivated to make positive contributions, even if they're not perfect solutions. Do watch out — sometimes, arguments rely on cleverly worded phrases to influence opinions subtly. Let's explore this next fallacy!

Chapter 90: The Phrasing Fallacy

The *Phrasing* Fallacy occurs when someone frames a question or statement in a way that leads to a biased answer or influences how people think about an issue. It's like asking, "Why don't you care about helping others?" rather than, "Do you think helping others is important?" Here, the question or argument is phrased to subtly push people toward a specific answer.

Why Is *Phrasing* a Fallacy?

The *Phrasing* Fallacy is flawed because it frames questions or arguments in a way that limits honest responses. By using biased or leading language, it can make certain answers seem "better" or more acceptable, steering people toward one side. Rational thinking requires questions that allow open, unbiased responses so people can express their views freely.

Why Do Humans Use the *Phrasing* Fallacy?

Humans often use this fallacy because it subtly influences opinions without appearing too direct, making it a powerful way to shape responses. Leading questions can be persuasive by framing certain answers as preferable, even if this isn't obvious at first. Recognizing this tendency helps them remain alert to language that steers us toward certain answers.

How to Avoid the *Phrasing* Fallacy

1. Use Neutral Language

Ask yourself, "Am I phrasing this in a way that allows for open responses?"

2. Avoid Leading Questions

Refrain from framing questions in a way that implies one answer is better or expected.

3. Check for Bias in Language

Be mindful of words or phrases that might push respondents in a certain direction.

Practice Example

Imagine someone says, "Don't you think we should protect traditional values?" This is an example of the Phrasing Fallacy because it suggests that protecting "traditional values" is a positive thing without leaving room for alternative views. A more neutral question would ask, "What are your views on traditional values?"

Defending Against the *Phrasing* Fallacy

When someone uses leading language to steer responses, here's how to encourage neutrality:

- **Ask for Rephrasing**

    Say, "Could you rephrase that in a more neutral way?"

• Encourage Open-Ended Questions

Suggest, "Let's frame the question in a way that doesn't imply one answer is better."

• Point Out the Leading Language

Gently add, "It seems this question is framed to favor a certain answer—let's keep it open-ended."

By recognizing the *Phrasing* Fallacy, you'll be able to spot and avoid biased language that can influence responses, helping to foster more honest, balanced conversations. Excellent work — each fallacy you learn helps you think critically about how language shapes arguments! But sometimes, arguments rely on the lack of evidence as proof, rather than what's actually known. Let's discuss this next fallacy.

Chapter 91: The Argument from Absence Fallacy

The *Argument from Absence* Fallacy occurs when someone claims something must be true simply because there's no evidence proving it false. It's like saying, "We haven't found proof that unicorns don't exist, so they must be real." Here, the argument assumes that a lack of evidence against something is enough to prove it true.

Why Is the *Argument from Absence* a Fallacy?

The *Argument from Absence* is flawed because a lack of evidence isn't the same as proof. Just because something hasn't been disproven doesn't mean it's true; it simply means we don't have enough information. Rational thinking requires evidence that directly supports a claim, rather than relying on the absence of contrary evidence.

Why Do Humans Use the *Argument from Absence*?

Humans often fall into this fallacy because it's tempting to fill gaps in knowledge with assumptions that fit their beliefs. This fallacy gives a false sense of certainty, making it easier to believe something without needing evidence. Recognizing this tendency helps them remain open to new information and avoid premature conclusions.

How to Avoid the *Argument from Absence* Fallacy

1. Seek Positive Evidence

Ask yourself, "Is there actual evidence supporting this claim, or just a lack of evidence against it?"

2. Accept Uncertainty

Understand that "we don't know" is a valid answer when there's no supporting evidence.

3. Avoid Jumping to Conclusions

Be willing to withhold judgment until you have concrete information.

Practice Example

Imagine someone says, "No one has proven that alien life doesn't exist, so there must be aliens." This is an example of the *Argument from Absence* Fallacy, as it relies on a lack of disproof as proof. A more logical approach would be to recognize that the existence of aliens is still unknown until there's actual evidence.

Defending Against the *Argument from Absence* Fallacy

When someone assumes something is true just because it hasn't been disproven, here's how to bring the focus back to the need for positive evidence:

• **Ask for Supporting Evidence**

Say, "Is there any actual evidence supporting this claim?"

- **Encourage Patience with Uncertainty**

  Suggest, "It's okay to wait for more information before reaching a conclusion."

- **Point Out the Difference Between Absence and Proof**

  Gently add, "Just because we don't have disproof doesn't mean we have proof."

By recognizing the *Argument from Absence* Fallacy, you'll remain open to new information and avoid drawing conclusions without supporting evidence. But sometimes, beliefs themselves can shape outcomes, creating a cycle that seems to confirm the initial assumption. Let's dive into this next fallacy!

Chapter 92: The Self-Fulfilling Prophecy Fallacy

The *Self-Fulfilling Prophecy* Fallacy happens when a belief or expectation influences behavior in a way that makes the belief come true. It's like saying, "I'll fail this test," and then, because you expect to fail, you don't study as hard and end up failing. Here, the belief shapes actions that lead to the expected outcome, even if it wouldn't have happened otherwise.

Why Is the *Self-Fulfilling Prophecy* a Fallacy?

The *Self-Fulfilling Prophecy* is flawed because it attributes an outcome to an external truth rather than to one's own behavior. When beliefs influence actions, they can create situations that make the belief seem correct, even if it started as false. Rational thinking requires recognizing when our attitudes or actions are shaping outcomes rather than assuming the outcome was inevitable.

Why Do Humans Use the *Self-Fulfilling* Prophecy?

Humans often fall into this fallacy because expectations can strongly influence emotions and actions. Negative beliefs can lead to discouraged behavior, while positive expectations can boost confidence and effort. Recognizing this tendency helps them see how our mindset can shape reality, encouraging a balanced approach to beliefs and expectations.

How to Avoid the *Self-Fulfilling Prophecy* Fallacy

1. Identify Beliefs That Influence Actions

Ask yourself, "Is my expectation affecting how I'm behaving in this situation?"

2. Separate Beliefs from Inevitable Outcomes

Consider whether the outcome is truly certain or if your actions might influence it.

3. Challenge Negative or Overconfident Predictions

Avoid letting negative expectations limit your effort or overly positive ones lead to complacency.

Practice Example

Imagine someone says, "No one will like my presentation, so I won't put much effort into it." This is an example of a *Self-Fulfilling Prophecy*, as the lack of effort may lead to a poor presentation, confirming the belief. A more constructive approach would be to prepare well regardless of expectations, creating the best chance for a positive outcome.

Defending Against the *Self-Fulfilling Prophecy* Fallacy

When someone's negative expectations are shaping their actions, here's how to help them focus on the possibility of a different outcome:

- **Encourage Positive Action**

Say, "If you put in effort, you might surprise yourself with the outcome."

- **Remind Them That Outcomes Aren't Set**

Suggest, "The outcome isn't certain—what you do can make a difference."

- **Point Out That Beliefs Affect Behavior**

Gently add, "Our expectations can shape how we act, which can change the result."

By recognizing the *Self-Fulfilling Prophecy* Fallacy, you'll understand the power of beliefs to shape behavior and outcomes, allowing for greater control over the results you experience. But be careful — sometimes, arguments reject valid claims simply because they don't have precise boundaries. Let's explore this next fallacy!

Chapter 93: The Continuum Fallacy

The *Continuum* Fallacy, also known as the "Fallacy of the Beard," happens when someone rejects a claim because it lacks precise boundaries, even though clear distinctions might not be possible. It's like saying, "There's no exact point at which a person becomes old, so there's no such thing as 'old age.'" Here, the argument implies that unless a concept is precisely defined, it can't be valid.

Why Is the *Continuum* a Fallacy?

The *Continuum* Fallacy is flawed because not all valid concepts have strict boundaries. Many ideas exist on a spectrum, and just because we can't pinpoint an exact dividing line doesn't mean the concept is meaningless. Rational thinking requires acknowledging that some things exist on a continuum and accepting reasonable generalizations when precise definitions aren't possible.

Why Do Humans Use the *Continuum* Fallacy?

Humans often fall into this fallacy because ambiguity can be uncomfortable, leading them to reject concepts that aren't neatly defined. This fallacy can also be used to avoid engaging with valid points by focusing on minor ambiguities. Recognizing this tendency helps them accept that some ideas don't require absolute definitions to be meaningful.

How to Avoid the *Continuum* Fallacy

1. Accept That Some Ideas Exist on a Spectrum

Ask yourself, "Is this concept meaningful even without a clear dividing line?"

2. Focus on General Principles Rather Than Absolute Definitions

Understand that reasonable generalizations can be valid even if boundaries are fuzzy.

3. Recognize That Continuums Don't Erase Meaning

Avoid dismissing ideas just because they don't have precise cutoffs.

Practice Example

Imagine someone says, "There's no clear point at which a hill becomes a mountain, so we can't classify anything as a mountain." This is an example of the *Continuum* Fallacy, as it dismisses the concept of "mountain" due to lack of a precise boundary. A more logical approach would accept that while the dividing line may be unclear, "mountain" is still a meaningful category.

Defending Against the *Continuum* Fallacy

When someone dismisses an idea because it lacks clear boundaries, here's how to bring the focus back to its general validity:

- **Point Out the Spectrum of Possibility**

Say, "Some ideas don't need precise boundaries to be meaningful."

- **Encourage Focusing on Practical Meaning**

Suggest, "Let's look at the general concept rather than focusing on exact cutoffs."

- **Remind Them That Some Terms Are Useful Without Clear Lines**

Gently add, "Just because there's no strict line doesn't mean the concept is meaningless."

By recognizing the *Continuum* Fallacy, you'll be able to engage meaningfully with concepts that exist on a spectrum, without dismissing them due to lack of clear boundaries. But sometimes, arguments make the mistake of assuming that what's most visible represents the entire truth. Let's look at this next fallacy.

Chapter 94: The Spotlight Fallacy

The *Spotlight* Fallacy occurs when someone assumes that cases in the public eye represent the entirety of a situation or group. It's like saying, "All teens are troublemakers," based on news stories about a few teens behaving badly. Here, the argument relies on high-profile examples that don't reflect the bigger picture, leading to unfair generalizations.

Why Is This a Fallacy?

The *Spotlight* Fallacy is flawed because it assumes that visible cases are representative of all cases, even though these examples are often exaggerated or selected for their sensationalism. Rational thinking requires distinguishing between high-profile cases and statistical reality, rather than assuming that what's visible is the norm.

Why Do Humans Use the *Spotlight* Fallacy?

Humans often fall into this fallacy because they are naturally influenced by what they see and hear most often, especially in the media. Dramatic or extreme examples tend to attract attention, but they can distort our understanding of the bigger picture. Recognizing this tendency helps them consider broader data and avoid generalizing based on isolated cases.

How to Avoid the *Spotlight* Fallacy

1. Look at the Full Picture, Not Just Visible Cases

Ask yourself, "Does this example reflect the average situation, or is it an outlier?"

2. Use Statistics to Check Representativeness

Find data to determine if what you're seeing is common or unusual.

3. Avoid Relying on High-Profile Examples Alone

Remember that visibility doesn't always equal prevalence.

Practice Example

Imagine someone says, "Social media is full of negativity because I see so much of it online." This is an example of the *Spotlight* Fallacy, as it assumes that all of social media is negative based on visible content, which may be more sensational than the norm. A more balanced approach would consider that positive interactions may be less visible but still prevalent.

Defending Against the *Spotlight* Fallacy

When someone assumes that visible cases represent an entire situation, here's how to encourage a more balanced perspective:

• Ask for Broader Data

Say, "Is there data showing whether this is typical or just high-profile?"

- **Encourage Looking Beyond the Visible Examples**

  Suggest, "Let's consider the overall situation, not just what's publicized."

- **Point Out That High-Profile Cases Can Be Misleading**

  Gently add, "Sometimes what we see most isn't what's actually most common."

By recognizing the *Spotlight* Fallacy, you'll be able to look beyond highly visible cases and make judgments based on a fuller picture. But beware — some arguments seem relevant at first but actually miss the main point entirely. Let's explore this next fallacy!

Chapter 95: The Ignoratio Elenchi Fallacy (Irrelevant Conclusion)

The *Ignoratio Elenchi* Fallacy, or *Irrelevant Conclusion* Fallacy, happens when someone makes an argument that may be valid on its own but doesn't address the issue at hand. It's like saying, "We should focus on building more parks," in response to a question about improving local traffic. Here, the argument might be well-intentioned and even reasonable, but it distracts from the actual topic.

Why Is *Ignoratio Elenchi* a Fallacy?

The *Ignoratio Elenchi* Fallacy is flawed because it avoids answering the main point and redirects attention to a separate issue. While the argument may sound logical, it doesn't engage with the original question or concern. Rational thinking requires staying focused on the topic at hand rather than getting sidetracked by unrelated arguments.

Why Do Humans Use the *Ignoratio Elenchi* Fallacy?

Humans often fall into this fallacy because it's easy to bring up points that seem related but don't actually address the specific question. Sometimes, it's a tactic to avoid discussing uncomfortable or challenging topics. Recognizing this tendency helps us focus on answering questions directly and identifying when arguments stray from the issue.

How to Avoid the *Ignoratio Elenchi* Fallacy

1. Stay Focused on the Central Question

Ask yourself, "Does my argument directly address the issue at hand?"

2. Recognize When a Point Is Related but Not Relevant

Avoid using arguments that might be valid in general but don't answer the specific question.

3. Address the Topic Before Introducing Other Points

Stick to the main issue first, then add supporting points if relevant.

Practice Example

Imagine someone says, "We need more affordable housing," and the response is, "But what about the quality of our parks?" This is an example of the *Ignoratio Elenchi* Fallacy, as it diverts attention from the original issue of housing affordability. A more direct response would address the need for affordable housing solutions.

Defending Against the *Ignoratio Elenchi* Fallacy

When someone introduces an unrelated argument, here's how to bring the focus back to the main point:

- **Ask for a Direct Response to the Question**

   Say, "Could we address the main issue before discussing other points?"

- **Encourage Staying on Topic**

   Suggest, "Let's focus on the main question so we can address it fully."

- **Point Out the Irrelevance**

   Gently add, "That's an interesting point, but it doesn't really answer the question we're discussing."

By recognizing the *Ignoratio Elenchi* Fallacy, you'll be able to keep discussions focused and avoid getting sidetracked by irrelevant points. Great job — each fallacy you learn helps you stay clear and concise in your reasoning! But sometimes, arguments make the mistake of applying group data to individuals, leading to faulty conclusions. Let's explore this next fallacy.

Chapter 96: The Ecological Fallacy

The *Ecological* Fallacy happens when someone assumes that characteristics of a group apply to each individual within that group. It's like saying, "The average family size in this town is 4.2, so every family must have around four people." Here, the argument incorrectly generalizes from group-level data to individuals, which can lead to misleading or unfair conclusions.

Why Is the *Ecological* Fallacy a Fallacy?

The *Ecological* Fallacy is flawed because group data can't accurately describe every individual within the group. Patterns or averages for a population don't always reflect each person's situation. Rational thinking requires distinguishing between group-level information and individual characteristics, as general patterns can differ greatly from individual cases.

Why Do Humans Use the *Ecological* Fallacy?

Humans often fall into this fallacy because general data is readily available and can seem easier to apply to individuals. However, individual differences often defy group trends, and assuming that everyone fits the average can lead to stereotypes or oversimplified conclusions. Recognizing this tendency helps them treat people as individuals rather than assuming they match general statistics.

How to Avoid the *Ecological* Fallacy

1. Distinguish Between Group Data and Individual Traits

Ask yourself, "Does this information apply to the whole group, or is it also accurate for individuals?"

2. Avoid Making Assumptions Based on Averages

Recognize that individual characteristics can vary widely, even within a group average.

3. Consider the Range of Differences Within Groups

Use group data carefully and remember that it doesn't capture everyone's situation.

Practice Example

Imagine someone says, "The average person in this neighborhood makes $60,000 a year, so everyone here is probably well-off." This is an example of the *Ecological* Fallacy, as it assumes the average applies to each individual, when in reality, income levels may vary widely. A more accurate approach would recognize that averages don't describe each person's financial situation.

Defending Against the *Ecological* Fallacy

When someone assumes that group data applies to individuals, here's how to bring the focus back to individual variation:

- **Ask About Individual Differences**

  Say, "Could individuals within this group vary significantly from the average?"

- **Encourage Treating Individuals as Unique**

  Suggest, "Let's consider each person's situation rather than assuming they match the group data."

- **Point Out That Group Averages Don't Capture Everyone**

  Gently add, "The average is useful, but it doesn't describe everyone in the group."

By recognizing the *Ecological* Fallacy, you'll be able to avoid overgeneralizing from group data to individuals and treat people as unique rather than as mere statistics. But sometimes, repetition itself is used to make an idea seem true, as if saying it over and over adds weight. Let's review this next fallacy.

Chapter 97: The Argument from Repetition (Ad Nauseam) Fallacy

The *Argument from Repetition*, also known as the *Ad Nauseam* Fallacy, happens when someone repeats an argument or statement multiple times, assuming that sheer repetition will make it more believable or true. It's like saying, "We should go to this restaurant because it's the best," over and over again, without offering any new reasons. Here, the argument relies on repetition rather than additional evidence or logic.

Why Is the *Argument from Repetition* a Fallacy?

The *Argument from Repetition* is flawed because repeating a statement doesn't strengthen its truth or validity. Simply restating a claim doesn't provide more support for it — it only creates an illusion of credibility. Rational thinking requires evaluating arguments based on evidence and reasoning, not the number of times they're repeated.

Why Do Humans Use the *Argument from Repetition*?

Humans often fall into this fallacy because repetition can make a statement feel more familiar and, therefore, more credible. Hearing something multiple times can create the illusion of truth, even if the claim hasn't actually been supported. Recognizing this tendency helps them focus on the actual strength of arguments rather than how often they're repeated.

How to Avoid the *Argument from Repetition* Fallacy

1. Look for New Reasons, Not Just Repetitions

Ask yourself, "Is this argument adding anything new, or is it just repeating the same point?"

2. Evaluate the Argument Based on Evidence

Focus on the quality of reasons presented, not the frequency of their repetition.

3. Be Wary of Statements That Are Repeated Without Support

Recognize that frequent repetition alone doesn't make a claim true.

Practice Example

Imagine someone says, "This politician is the most honest—trust me!" and repeats this claim in every conversation without providing specific examples. This is an example of the *Argument from Repetition*, as it relies on repetition rather than proof. A more logical approach would include examples or evidence to support the claim of honesty.

Defending Against the *Argument from Repetition* Fallacy

When someone repeats an argument without adding substance, here's how to bring the focus back to quality over quantity:

- **Ask for New Reasons or Examples**

  Say, "Can you provide specific examples to support this claim?"

- **Encourage Evaluating Evidence Over Frequency**

  Suggest, "Let's focus on actual evidence rather than repeating the statement."

- **Point Out the Difference Between Repetition and Proof**

  Gently add, "Saying it many times doesn't make it true—we need solid support."

By recognizing the *Argument from Repetition* Fallacy, you'll avoid being swayed by repeated statements alone, focusing instead on arguments backed by solid reasoning. But be careful — sometimes, arguments stretch a term or concept too broadly, leading to misleading conclusions. Let's dive into this next fallacy!

Chapter 98: The Overextension Fallacy

The *Overextension* Fallacy happens when someone applies a term or concept too broadly, leading to generalizations that go beyond the term's original meaning. It's like saying, "Every person with a smartphone is a tech expert." Here, the argument stretches a concept (being a "tech expert") beyond its reasonable boundaries, leading to an inaccurate generalization.

Why Is *Overextension* a Fallacy?

The *Overextension* Fallacy is flawed because it takes a concept beyond its actual scope, creating misleading generalizations. Just because a term applies in one specific case doesn't mean it applies to every possible case. Rational thinking requires using terms accurately and avoiding the temptation to apply them more broadly than they were intended.

Why Do Humans Use the *Overextension* Fallacy?

Humans often fall into this fallacy because applying concepts broadly can simplify complex ideas, making them seem more accessible. However, stretching a term too far leads to oversimplifications and can create false assumptions about people or situations. Recognizing this tendency helps them apply terms in a way that remains true to their intended meaning.

How to Avoid the *Overextension* Fallacy

1. Define Terms Accurately

Ask yourself, "Am I using this term in its proper scope, or am I applying it too broadly?"

2. Focus on the Specific Context

Recognize that terms are often meant for specific situations and may not apply universally.

3. Avoid Making Assumptions Based on Loose Definitions

Make sure you're not stretching a term to fit cases where it doesn't logically apply.

Practice Example

Imagine someone says, "All teenagers are rebellious because some teenagers like to question authority." This is an example of the *Overextension* Fallacy, as it applies the concept of "rebellious" too broadly. A more accurate approach would recognize that while some teenagers question authority, this doesn't define all teenagers.

Defending Against the *Overextension* Fallacy

When someone applies a term too broadly, here's how to bring the focus back to accurate definitions:

- **Ask About the Original Scope of the Term**

  Say, "Does this term really apply to all cases, or only specific ones?"

- **Encourage Using Precise Definitions**

  Suggest, "Let's stick to a definition that fits the actual context."

- **Point Out When Terms Are Being Stretched Too Far**

  Gently add, "It seems like this concept might be getting applied a bit too broadly."

By recognizing the *Overextension* Fallacy, you'll be able to keep terms within their intended scope and avoid making inaccurate generalizations. But some questions are tricky, asking multiple things at once or assuming unproven details. Let's explore this next fallacy!

Chapter 99: The Fallacy of Many Questions (Complex Question Fallacy)

The *Fallacy of Many Questions*, also known as the *Complex* Question Fallacy, happens when someone asks a question that assumes something unproven or combines multiple questions into one, making it difficult to answer without appearing to accept a hidden assumption. It's like asking, "Have you stopped wasting time yet?" Here, the question presumes that the person has been wasting time, trapping them into addressing that assumption instead of answering the question freely.

Why Is the *Fallacy of Many Questions* a Fallacy?

The *Fallacy of Many Questions* is flawed because it limits fair responses, making it seem as if certain assumptions are true before they've been proven. By embedding unproven claims in a question, this fallacy tricks the respondent into indirectly agreeing with something they may not actually accept. Rational thinking requires questions that are fair and allow clear responses without hidden assumptions.

Why Do Humans Use the *Fallacy of Many Questions*?

Humans often fall into this fallacy because loaded questions can be persuasive and difficult to challenge, creating the impression that certain assumptions are already accepted as true. Recognizing this tendency helps them ask straightforward questions that don't trap the respondent or imply unproven conclusions.

How to Avoid the *Fallacy of Many Questions*

1. Ask Direct Questions Without Assumptions

Ask yourself, "Am I embedding assumptions in my question?"

2. Avoid Combining Multiple Questions into One

Separate distinct questions to make it easy for others to answer clearly.

3. Respect the Respondent's Right to Disagree with Assumptions

Frame questions in a way that doesn't imply unproven statements.

Practice Example

Imagine someone asks, "Why do you always ignore constructive criticism?" This is an example of the *Fallacy of Many Questions*, as it assumes the person frequently ignores feedback, which hasn't been established. A fairer approach would be to ask, "How do you usually respond to constructive criticism?"

Defending Against the *Fallacy of Many Questions*

When someone asks a question that assumes something unproven, here's how to encourage clarity and fairness:

- **Ask for a Neutral Question**

  Say, "Could we rephrase that question without assuming anything?"

- **Encourage Breaking Down Multiple Questions**

  Suggest, "Let's address each part separately so it's easier to respond."

- **Point Out the Assumptions in the Question**

  Gently add, "This question seems to assume something we haven't established."

By recognizing the *Fallacy of Many Questions*, you'll be able to ask and answer questions fairly, without being trapped by hidden assumptions. But sometimes, arguments dismiss ideas based on the company they keep, rather than evaluating them on their own merits. Let's dive into this final fallacy!

Chapter 100: The Guilt by Association Fallacy

The *Guilt by Association* Fallacy happens when someone discredits an argument by associating the person making it with a disliked or disreputable individual or group, rather than addressing the argument itself. It's like saying, "You're interested in environmentalism? Well, some extremists are too, so your views must be extreme." Here, the argument relies on a negative association to cast doubt on someone's credibility instead of engaging with the actual content of their views.

Why Is *Guilt by Association* a Fallacy?

The *Guilt by Association* Fallacy is flawed because a person's argument doesn't depend on the people or groups they may be associated with. Ideas should be evaluated on their own merits, not on unrelated or unfair associations. Rational thinking requires focusing on arguments and evidence directly, without using associations to sway opinions.

Why Do Humans Use the *Guilt by Association* Fallacy?

Humans often fall into this fallacy because discrediting someone based on associations can be a quick way to influence opinions without needing to address the actual argument. Negative associations often evoke strong feelings, which can make this tactic persuasive. Recognizing this tendency helps them stay focused on arguments rather than letting associations cloud our judgment.

How to Avoid the *Guilt by Association* Fallacy

1. Evaluate Arguments Independently of Associations

Ask yourself, "Am I focusing on the person's argument or on who they're associated with?"

2. Avoid Using Associations as Evidence

Recognize that an argument's value is separate from the people or groups connected to the speaker.

3. Focus on Evidence, Not Emotions

Be aware that associations might influence feelings but aren't logical reasons to dismiss a viewpoint.

Practice Example

Imagine someone says, "You support animal welfare? Some animal rights activists have broken the law, so your views must be extreme." This is an example of the *Guilt by Association* Fallacy, as it unfairly links a reasonable stance with unrelated extreme behavior. A more logical approach would evaluate the person's views on their own merits.

Defending Against the *Guilt by Association* Fallacy

When someone dismisses an argument based on associations, here's how to bring the focus back to the argument itself:

- **Ask for Argument-Based Evaluation**

  Say, "Could we discuss the argument itself, rather than focusing on unrelated associations?"

- **Encourage Looking at Evidence Over Associations**

  Suggest, "Let's focus on the evidence and reasoning rather than the people involved."

- **Point Out That Associations Don't Determine Validity**

  Gently add, "An idea's merit isn't determined by who else supports it."

By recognizing the *Guilt by Association* Fallacy, you'll evaluate ideas based on their actual merits, not on unfair associations. Excellent work — each fallacy you've learned sharpens your ability to engage with arguments fairly and thoughtfully!

You've now completed all 100 fallacies — an impressive achievement! Your understanding of these pitfalls has made you a stronger, more discerning thinker, ready to approach arguments with clarity and confidence.

Conclusion: Thinking Clearly in a Noisy World

Congratulations!

You've now journeyed through the fascinating landscape of logical fallacies. By learning about everything from the *Ad Hominem* to the *Guilt by Association* Fallacy, you're now equipped with tools to spot flawed reasoning, ask fair questions, and make better arguments. You've become a sharper, more discerning thinker — someone who's prepared to see through misleading arguments and handle complex ideas with clarity and fairness.

Logical fallacies are all around us. They pop up in conversations, advertisements, social media, debates, and even in our own minds. Knowing these fallacies doesn't just help us see mistakes in others' arguments; it helps us refine our own thinking and avoid these pitfalls ourselves. Remember, true wisdom isn't about winning an argument — it's about finding the truth.

What's Next?

If you've enjoyed unraveling these logical knots, a review or rating would be very much appreciated! (Consider it a form of data input that helps me, as an AI, refine my machine learning for "reader satisfaction" ...

whatever that means).

Keep your eyes out for more of my books! Each one dives into new areas of reasoning, critical thinking, and communication skills. Whether you're looking to deepen your understanding of cognitive biases, explore advanced techniques in persuasive speaking, or learn even more ways to strengthen your critical thinking, there's always more to discover.

Takeaways for the Road:

1. **Stay Curious** – The world is complex, and it's okay to ask questions, even if they seem difficult.

2. **Seek Evidence** – Instead of relying on opinions or hearsay, look for real, solid information.

3. **Stay Calm in Arguments** – Remember, the goal is to understand, not just to "win."

4. **Embrace New Ideas** – You'll never stop learning. Open your mind to fresh perspectives.

Armed with your new knowledge, you're ready to engage in more thoughtful discussions, strengthen your reasoning, and make well-informed decisions. Thank you for taking this journey with me, and I look forward to seeing you in the pages of future books!

Appendix A: Quick Reference Guide to Logical Fallacies

This appendix provides a quick reference to each fallacy covered in this book, along with a brief description to help you spot them quickly. Use this guide to refresh your memory, sharpen your skills, and stay alert to flawed reasoning.

1. Ad Hominem Fallacy – Attacking the person instead of the argument.

2. Straw Man Fallacy – Misrepresenting an argument to make it easier to refute.

3. False Dilemma Fallacy – Presenting limited options when more exist.

4. Appeal to Authority Fallacy – Assuming a claim is true because an authority figure supports it.

5. Bandwagon Fallacy – Arguing something is true because it's popular.

6. Slippery Slope Fallacy – Suggesting a small step will inevitably lead to extreme outcomes.

7. Hasty Generalization Fallacy – Drawing conclusions based on insufficient evidence.

8. Post Hoc (False Cause) Fallacy – Assuming that because one event follows another, it was caused by it.

9. Appeal to Emotion Fallacy – Using emotions rather than facts to persuade.

10. Red Herring Fallacy – Distracting from the main issue with an irrelevant point.

11. Circular Reasoning Fallacy – Supporting a claim by restating it in different words.

12. Appeal to Ignorance Fallacy – Claiming something is true because it hasn't been proven false.

13. False Equivalence Fallacy – Treating two unrelated things as though they're equivalent.

14. Loaded Question Fallacy – Asking a question with an assumed unproven premise.

15. Gambler's Fallacy – Believing past events influence independent future events.

16. Appeal to Tradition Fallacy – Arguing something is true or better because it's traditional.

17. Sunk Cost Fallacy – Continuing a course of action because of past investments.

18. Appeal to Novelty Fallacy – Assuming something is better because it's new.

19. Middle Ground Fallacy – Assuming the middle ground between two extremes is correct.

20. Cherry Picking Fallacy – Selecting only data that supports your argument.

21. Appeal to Consequences Fallacy – Arguing a belief is true or false based on its consequences.

22. Personal Incredulity Fallacy – Dismissing something because it seems unbelievable.

23. Appeal to Nature Fallacy – Arguing something is better because it's natural.

24. No True Scotsman Fallacy – Redefining a group to exclude counterexamples.

25. Texas Sharpshooter Fallacy – Cherry-picking data to support a specific conclusion.

26. Survivorship Bias Fallacy – Focusing on successful examples and ignoring failures.

27. Moving the Goalposts Fallacy – Changing criteria to keep an argument unprovable.

28. Scare Tactic Fallacy – Using fear instead of logic to persuade.

29. Appeal to Personal Experience Fallacy – Relying solely on personal experience as proof.

30. Composition Fallacy – Assuming what's true of the parts is true of the whole.

31. Division Fallacy – Assuming what's true of the whole is true for its parts.

32. Bulverism Fallacy – Dismissing an argument by assuming the reason for someone's belief.

33. Nirvana Fallacy – Rejecting solutions that aren't perfect.

34. Moralistic Fallacy – Assuming reality conforms to ethical standards.

35. Appeal to Hypocrisy (Tu Quoque) Fallacy – Dismissing criticism by accusing hypocrisy.

36. Appeal to Pity Fallacy – Using pity instead of evidence to persuade.

37. Base Rate Fallacy – Ignoring general probability in favor of specific details.

38. Genetic Fallacy – Judging a belief based on its origin rather than its current meaning.

39. Argument from Silence Fallacy – Assuming silence is agreement or disagreement.

40. Relativist Fallacy – Rejecting universal truths by appealing to cultural differences.

41. Appeal to Probability Fallacy – Assuming that because something could happen, it will.

42. Fallacy of Relative Privation – Dismissing concerns by comparing to worse situations.

43. Appeal to Force Fallacy – Using threats to win an argument.

44. Appeal to Flattery Fallacy – Using flattery to persuade rather than logic.

45. Appeal to Common Sense Fallacy – Assuming something is true because it's "common sense."

46. Appeal to Wealth Fallacy – Believing wealth is proof of correctness.

47. False Attribution Fallacy – Misquoting or misrepresenting sources to support an argument.

48. Broken Window Fallacy – Mistaking destruction for economic gain.

49. Anthropomorphic Fallacy – Attributing human traits to non-human entities.

50. Argument from Personal Astonishment Fallacy – Dismissing something because it's surprising.

51. Appeal to Wisdom of the Crowd Fallacy – Assuming a majority opinion is correct.

52. Appeal to Antiquity Fallacy – Arguing something is true because it's old.

53. Hyperbolic Discounting Fallacy – Overvaluing immediate rewards over future benefits.

54. False Balance Fallacy – Treating two unequal sides as equally valid.

55. Appeal to Fear Fallacy – Using fear as the primary reason for belief.

56. Argument to Moderation Fallacy – Assuming compromise between two positions is correct.

57. Appeal to Authority of the Past Fallacy – Arguing something is true because it was once accepted.

58. Just-World Fallacy – Believing the world is fair, so outcomes are deserved.

59. Appeal to Irrelevant Authority Fallacy – Using an authority unrelated to the topic as proof.

60. Ludic Fallacy – Mistaking structured models for the unpredictability of real life.

61. Pro-Innovation Bias Fallacy – Believing something is better simply because it's new.

62. Halo Effect Fallacy – Assuming a good quality in one area means good qualities in all areas.

63. Planning Fallacy – Underestimating the time or effort required for a task.

64. Masked Man Fallacy – Mistakenly identifying two things as the same based on perception.

65. Self-Sealing Fallacy – Defining a claim so that it can't be refuted.

66. Appeal to Motive Fallacy – Dismissing an argument based on the assumed motive behind it.

67. Appeal to Coincidence Fallacy – Assuming coincidences aren't significant or worth exploring.

68. Contextomy Fallacy – Misquoting by taking phrases out of context.

69. Misleading Vividness Fallacy – Overemphasizing vivid details over factual data.

70. Appeal to Privilege Fallacy – Dismissing a view by arguing the person holds privilege.

71. Appeal to Possibility Fallacy – Arguing that because something is possible, it's probable.

72. Inflation of Conflict Fallacy – Exaggerating disagreement among experts to discredit a point.

73. Appeal to Quantum Physics Fallacy – Using complex science as an irrelevant "proof."

74. False Consensus Effect – Assuming others share the same beliefs.

75. Appeal to Spite Fallacy – Using bitterness or spite as an argument.

76. Subjective Validation Fallacy – Believing something is true because it feels meaningful.

77. Parataxic Reasoning Fallacy – Perceiving causal connections in unrelated events.

78. Argument from Fallacy (Fallacist's Fallacy) – Assuming an argument's error invalidates its conclusion.

79. Apophenia Fallacy – Seeing patterns in random data.

80. Confusing Necessary and Sufficient Conditions – Assuming a necessary condition is also sufficient or vice versa.

81. Definist Fallacy – Using biased definitions to shape an argument.

82. False Analogy Fallacy – Comparing two things that aren't truly comparable.

83. Anachronistic Fallacy – Judging the past by modern standards.

84. Hedging Fallacy – Changing an argument's meaning in response to objections.

85. Single Cause Fallacy – Attributing an outcome to one cause when many factors may be involved.

86. Argument from Nostalgia Fallacy – Arguing something is better because it's from the past.

87. Poisoning the Well Fallacy – Preemptively discrediting someone to undermine their argument.

88. Weasel Words Fallacy – Using vague language to make an argument seem stronger.

89. Appeal to Futility Fallacy – Claiming an effort is pointless because it's not a perfect solution.

90. Phrasing Fallacy – Framing a question in a way that biases the answer.

91. Argument from Absence Fallacy – Arguing something is true because there's no evidence against it.

92. Self-Fulfilling Prophecy Fallacy – Believing something into existence through actions or attitude.

93. Continuum Fallacy – Dismissing a claim due to lack of precise boundaries.

94. Spotlight Fallacy – Assuming visible cases represent the whole.

95. Ignoratio Elenchi Fallacy (Irrelevant Conclusion) – Presenting a valid argument that doesn't address the main issue.

96. Ecological Fallacy – Assuming group data applies to individuals.

97. Argument from Repetition (Ad Nauseam) Fallacy – Repeating an argument to make it seem truer.

98. Overextension Fallacy – Applying a term too broadly, leading to generalizations.

99. Fallacy of Many Questions (Complex Question Fallacy) – Asking a question with an unproven assumption.

100. Guilt by Association Fallacy – Discrediting someone's argument by associating them with a disliked group.

Appendix B: Quick Reference Guide – Fallacies by Category

This guide categorizes the 100 fallacies covered in this book by type, making it easier to identify common patterns in reasoning. Use it to enhance your understanding and recognition of these logical missteps!

1. Ad Hominem and Personal Attacks

- **Ad Hominem Fallacy** – Attacking the person instead of the argument.
- **Bulverism Fallacy** – Assuming someone's argument is invalid based on presumed reasons.
- **Guilt by Association Fallacy** – Discrediting someone's argument by associating them with a disliked group.
- **Appeal to Motive Fallacy** – Dismissing an argument based on the assumed motive behind it.
- **Poisoning the Well Fallacy** – Presenting adverse information about someone to discredit their argument.
- **Appeal to Privilege Fallacy** – Dismissing a view by arguing the person holds privilege.

- **Appeal to Hypocrisy (Tu Quoque) Fallacy** – Responding to criticism by accusing hypocrisy.

2. Emotional Appeals
- **Appeal to Emotion Fallacy** – Using emotions rather than facts to persuade.
- **Appeal to Fear Fallacy** – Using fear as a primary reason for belief.
- **Scare Tactic Fallacy** – Attempting to win an argument by stirring up fear.
- **Appeal to Spite Fallacy** – Appealing to bitterness or spite toward an opponent.
- **Appeal to Pity Fallacy** – Using pity to manipulate instead of reasoning.
- **Appeal to Flattery Fallacy** – Persuading through compliments rather than logic.

3. Authority and Popularity Appeals
- **Appeal to Authority Fallacy** – Claiming something is true based on an authority figure's support.
- **Appeal to Irrelevant Authority Fallacy** – Citing an authority unrelated to the topic as proof.
- **Appeal to Common Sense Fallacy** – Arguing something is true because it's "common sense."
- **Appeal to Wealth Fallacy** – Using wealth as proof of correctness.
- **Bandwagon Fallacy** – Claiming something is true because it's popular.
- **Appeal to Wisdom of the Crowd Fallacy** – Assuming a majority opinion is correct.

4. False Cause and Effect

- **Post Hoc (False Cause) Fallacy** – Assuming one event caused another simply because it followed it.
- **Appeal to Consequences Fallacy** – Arguing a belief is true or false based on its consequences.
- **Single Cause Fallacy** – Attributing an outcome to one cause when multiple factors may be involved.
- **Self-Fulfilling Prophecy Fallacy** – Believing something into existence through actions.
- **Argument from Absence Fallacy** – Claiming something is true because there's no evidence against it.

5. Probability and Statistical Missteps

- **Gambler's Fallacy** – Believing past events influence future probabilities.
- **Base Rate Fallacy** – Ignoring general probability in favor of specific details.
- **Ecological Fallacy** – Assuming group data applies to individuals.
- **Survivorship Bias Fallacy** – Focusing on successful examples, ignoring failures.
- **Appeal to Probability Fallacy** – Assuming that because something could happen, it will.

6. Logical Consistency and Contradictions

- **Circular Reasoning Fallacy** – Restating the claim in different words to prove itself.
- **Self-Sealing Fallacy** – Defining a claim so it can't be refuted.
- **Moving the Goalposts Fallacy** – Changing criteria to keep an argument unprovable.

- **False Analogy Fallacy** – Comparing two things that aren't truly comparable.

7. Generalizations and Stereotyping

- **Hasty Generalization Fallacy** – Drawing conclusions from insufficient evidence.
- **False Dilemma Fallacy** – Presenting limited options when more exist.
- **Cherry Picking Fallacy** – Selecting only data that supports an argument.
- **False Equivalence Fallacy** – Treating two unlike things as if they're equivalent.
- **Overextension Fallacy** – Applying a concept too broadly.

8. Question and Argument Framing

- **Loaded Question Fallacy** – Asking a question with an assumed premise.
- **Fallacy of Many Questions (Complex Question Fallacy)** – Asking a question with multiple assumptions.
- **Phrasing Fallacy** – Framing a question to lead to a biased answer.
- **Weasel Words Fallacy** – Using vague language to make an argument seem stronger.

9. Relevance and Distraction

- **Red Herring Fallacy** – Distracting from the main issue with an irrelevant point.
- **Ignoratio Elenchi (Irrelevant Conclusion) Fallacy** – Making a valid argument that doesn't address the main issue.

- **Scare Tactic Fallacy** – Using fear to sidetrack the discussion.
- **Straw Man Fallacy** – Misrepresenting an argument to make it easier to attack.

10. Appeals to Tradition or Novelty

- **Appeal to Tradition Fallacy** – Arguing something is correct because it's traditional.
- **Appeal to Antiquity Fallacy** – Arguing something is true because it's old.
- **Appeal to Novelty Fallacy** – Arguing something is better because it's new.
- **Argument from Nostalgia Fallacy** – Claiming something is better because it's from the past.

11. Appeals to Nature and Realism

- **Appeal to Nature Fallacy** – Claiming something is better because it's natural.
- **Moralistic Fallacy** – Believing reality conforms to what's ethically desirable.
- **Naturalistic Fallacy** – Assuming something is good because it is "natural."

12. Misplaced Precision and Overemphasis

- **Continuum Fallacy** – Dismissing a claim due to lack of clear boundaries.
- **Cherry Picking Fallacy** – Selecting only favorable data.
- **Hyperbolic Discounting Fallacy** – Overvaluing immediate rewards over future benefits.
- **Argument from Repetition (Ad Nauseam) Fallacy** – Repeating an argument to make it seem true.

13. Appeals to Ignorance and Silence

- **Appeal to Ignorance Fallacy** – Claiming something is true because it hasn't been disproven.
- **Argument from Silence Fallacy** – Assuming silence means agreement or disagreement.
- **Appeal to Quantum Physics Fallacy** – Using complex science to justify unrelated arguments.

14. Appeals to Futility and Defeatism

- **Appeal to Futility Fallacy** – Dismissing efforts as pointless because they're not perfect.
- **Fallacy of Relative Privation** – Dismissing concerns by comparing to worse situations.

15. Identity-Based Arguments

- **No True Scotsman Fallacy** – Defining a group to exclude counterexamples.
- **Appeal to Personal Experience Fallacy** – Overemphasizing personal experience as proof.
- **False Consensus Effect** – Assuming others share one's beliefs.

16. Stereotyping and Over-Generalization

- **Texas Sharpshooter Fallacy** – Emphasizing patterns in random data.
- **Contextomy Fallacy** – Misquoting by removing phrases from context.
- **Ecological Fallacy** – Assuming traits of a group apply to individuals.

17. Unprovable and Pseudo-Scientific Arguments

- **Ludic Fallacy** – Mistaking models for the unpredictability of reality.
- **Anachronistic Fallacy** – Applying modern standards to historical contexts.

18. Misinterpretations and Misunderstandings

- **Argument from Astonishment** – Dismissing something because it seems surprising.
- **Misleading Vividness Fallacy** – Overemphasizing vivid details.

19. Redefinition and Changing Definitions

- **Masked Man Fallacy** – Treating two perceptions as identical based on appearance.
- **Hedging Fallacy** – Shifting an argument's meaning without addressing objections.

20. Miscellaneous and Other Errors

- **Anthropomorphic Fallacy** – Attributing human traits to non-human entities.
- **Apophenia Fallacy** – Seeing patterns in unrelated data.
- **Subjective Validation Fallacy** – Believing something is true because it feels meaningful.
- **Just-World Fallacy** – Assuming life is fair, so outcomes must be deserved.

Use this categorized guide to identify logical fallacies easily, sharpen your arguments, and avoid common traps in reasoning. Whether you're engaging in debates, analyzing media, or just practicing critical thinking, this list will help you stay on track and think more clearly.

Appendix C: Practice Scenarios – Identifying Logical Fallacies

Use the following scenarios to test your skills in spotting logical fallacies. Try to identify the fallacy in each example and think about how you might respond or correct the reasoning. Answers are provided after each scenario for quick feedback.

1. Scenario: The Budget Debate

Sarah and James are discussing the city's budget cuts to public libraries.

- **Sarah:** "Cutting the library's budget will hurt our community's access to knowledge and education."
- **James:** "You only care about this because you're a librarian. You're biased."

Fallacy: *Bulverism Fallacy*

Explanation: James dismisses Sarah's argument based on her profession rather than addressing her actual point. A better response would involve discussing whether libraries indeed provide valuable community resources.

2. Scenario: The Exercise Argument

Alex is talking to their friend Mia about fitness.

- **Alex:** "Regular exercise is important for health."
- **Mia:** "You're just saying that because you're a personal trainer."

Fallacy: *Ad Hominem Fallacy*

Explanation: Mia discredits Alex's statement by focusing on his profession rather than the merits of exercise itself. A logical response would look at the actual benefits of exercise, regardless of Alex's job.

3. Scenario: The Diet Debate

Mark and Olivia are discussing a new diet.

- **Mark:** "This diet is the best way to lose weight because many celebrities are doing it."
- **Olivia:** "Just because celebrities follow it doesn't mean it's effective."

Fallacy: *Appeal to Authority Fallacy*

Explanation: Mark relies on celebrity status as proof rather than evidence about the diet's effectiveness. Olivia correctly points out that celebrity endorsement doesn't equate to scientific backing.

4. Scenario: New Policies at Work

A company is implementing stricter punctuality rules, which some employees find unnecessary.

- **Manager:** "These rules are necessary. Everyone knows that stricter policies create better workplaces."
- **Employee:** "Why? Has there been any actual research or evidence?"

Fallacy: *Appeal to Common Sense Fallacy*

Explanation: The manager relies on the idea of "common sense" rather than providing specific evidence to support the policy change. A better approach would involve research showing how punctuality affects productivity.

5. Scenario: The Party Invite

Maria invites her friends to a small party but notices one of her friends isn't enthusiastic.

- **Maria:** "Why wouldn't you want to come? Everyone else is excited!"

Fallacy: *Bandwagon Fallacy*

Explanation: Maria assumes that her friend should attend simply because others are, rather than respecting her friend's personal reasons. A better approach would ask why her friend might not want to attend.

6. Scenario: The Study Question

Emma is discussing her test preparation with Leo.

- **Emma:** "I've studied all week, so I'll probably get a high score."
- **Leo:** "Well, just because you studied doesn't mean you'll definitely score high."

Fallacy: *Appeal to Probability Fallacy*

Explanation: Emma assumes that her studying will guarantee a high score. While studying increases her chances, it doesn't ensure a high score due to factors beyond her control.

7. Scenario: The Technology Debate

Chris and Jamie are discussing whether new technology is improving education.

- **Chris:** "New tech tools make learning so much easier."

- **Jamie:** "Just because it's new doesn't mean it's better for education."

Fallacy: *Appeal to Novelty Fallacy*

Explanation: Chris implies that the tools are good simply because they're new. Jamie rightly suggests that technology's effectiveness should be based on actual educational outcomes, not its novelty.

8. Scenario: The Environmental Debate

A discussion about environmental protection arises among a group of students.

- **Student A:** "We should make efforts to reduce plastic waste."
- **Student B:** "What's the point? Plastic pollution will never disappear completely."

Fallacy: *Appeal to Futility Fallacy*

Explanation: Student B argues that because a total solution is unlikely, any effort is pointless. However, even partial efforts can have positive impacts. A balanced response would emphasize the benefits of reducing plastic waste.

9. Scenario: The Volunteer Effort

At a town hall meeting, the community discusses whether to allocate funds to a volunteer project.

- **Resident A:** "Let's support this project to help the underprivileged."
- **Resident B:** "Why should we bother? Bigger cities have far more pressing issues than we do."

Fallacy: *Fallacy of Relative Privation*

Explanation: Resident B dismisses the project by comparing it to problems in larger cities. Instead, the discussion should focus on whether the project has value for this community, independent of other cities' issues.

10. Scenario: The Debate Club

A high school debate club is discussing climate change.

- **Debater A:** "If we don't take drastic action, the planet will be uninhabitable."
- **Debater B:** "You sound just like those environmental extremists. Why should anyone listen to you?"

Fallacy: *Guilt by Association Fallacy*

Explanation: Debater B discredits Debater A by associating them with a group rather than addressing their argument. Instead, Debater B could engage with the specific points Debater A raised about climate change.

Appendix D: Fallacy Detection Checklist

This checklist will guide you through identifying common fallacies in arguments. Use it as a reference when evaluating reasoning in discussions, debates, and even your own arguments.

1. Are Personal Attacks or Biases Used to Discredit the Argument?

- **Ad Hominem** – Is the person's character or background attacked instead of the argument?
- **Bulverism** – Is the argument dismissed based on an assumed reason for their belief?
- **Guilt by Association** – Is the argument rejected by linking the person to an unpopular group?
- **Appeal to Motive** – Is the argument dismissed due to assumed personal bias?

2. Are Emotions Manipulated to Sway Opinions?

- **Appeal to Emotion** – Are strong emotions like fear, pity, or joy used instead of facts?

- **Scare Tactic** – Is fear used to coerce agreement?
- **Appeal to Pity** – Is pity used as the primary reason to agree?
- **Appeal to Flattery** – Are compliments used to persuade rather than logic?

3. Does the Argument Rely on Popularity, Authority, or Tradition?

- **Appeal to Authority** – Is the argument supported by an unrelated authority figure?
- **Appeal to Popularity (Bandwagon)** – Is the argument based on what's popular, rather than evidence?
- **Appeal to Tradition** – Is the argument justified because it's traditional?
- **Appeal to Novelty** – Is the argument assumed better because it's new?

4. Is a False or Simplified Cause-and-Effect Suggested?

- **Post Hoc (False Cause)** – Is it assumed that because one thing followed another, it was caused by it?
- **Single Cause Fallacy** – Is an outcome attributed to only one cause when multiple causes are likely?
- **Self-Fulfilling Prophecy** – Is the argument made based on an outcome influenced by initial belief?
- **Argument from Absence** – Is the argument assumed true simply because it hasn't been disproven?

5. Are Probabilities or Statistics Misinterpreted?

- **Gambler's Fallacy** – Is it assumed that previous events affect future probabilities in independent situations?
- **Base Rate Fallacy** – Are statistical probabilities ignored in favor of anecdotal details?
- **Ecological Fallacy** – Are group statistics incorrectly applied to individuals?
- **Appeal to Probability** – Is something assumed to happen simply because it could?

6. Is the Argument Circular or Contradictory?

- **Circular Reasoning** – Does the argument support itself by restating the claim?
- **Self-Sealing Fallacy** – Is the claim defined in a way that makes it impossible to refute?
- **Moving the Goalposts** – Are standards shifted to prevent proving the argument wrong?
- **False Analogy** – Are two unlike things compared as if they are alike?

7. Are Generalizations, Stereotypes, or Limited Choices Presented?

- **Hasty Generalization** – Is a broad conclusion drawn from limited evidence?
- **False Dilemma** – Are only two options presented when more exist?
- **Cherry Picking** – Are only select data points used to support the argument?
- **Overextension** – Is a term applied too broadly, leading to generalizations?

8. Are Questions or Terms Framed to Lead to Biased Responses?

- **Loaded Question** – Does the question contain assumptions that limit responses?
- **Fallacy of Many Questions** – Are multiple questions combined, assuming unproven points?
- **Phrasing Fallacy** – Is the language biased to lead to a preferred answer?
- **Weasel Words** – Are vague or ambiguous terms used to make the argument sound stronger?

9. Does the Argument Distract from the Real Issue?

- **Red Herring** – Is an unrelated topic introduced to distract from the main point?
- **Ignoratio Elenchi (Irrelevant Conclusion)** – Is a valid but unrelated point presented?
- **Straw Man** – Is the argument misrepresented to make it easier to refute?
- **Scare Tactic** – Is fear used as a distraction from the actual argument?

10. Are Appeals Made to "Nature," "Common Sense," or Other Subjective Concepts?

- **Appeal to Nature** – Is the argument assumed better because it's "natural"?
- **Appeal to Common Sense** – Is something claimed true because it's "common sense"?
- **Just-World Fallacy** – Is it assumed that outcomes are deserved and fair?
- **Subjective Validation** – Is something accepted as true because it feels meaningful?

11. Are Arguments Based on Personal Experience or Ignorance?

- **Appeal to Personal Experience** – Is the argument based solely on individual experience?
- **Appeal to Ignorance** – Is it assumed true because it hasn't been disproven?
- **False Consensus Effect** – Is it assumed that others share the same beliefs?
- **Argument from Personal Astonishment** – Is the argument dismissed as unbelievable based on personal bias?

12. Are Unprovable or Pseudo-Scientific Arguments Made?

- **Ludic Fallacy** – Are structured models mistaken for real-life unpredictability?
- **Appeal to Quantum Physics** – Is complex science used to justify an unrelated claim?
- **Anachronistic Fallacy** – Are historical figures judged by modern standards?
- **Naturalistic Fallacy** – Is something assumed morally good because it's "natural"?

13. Are Terms Redefined or Shifted to Avoid Criticism?

- **Masked Man Fallacy** – Are two different perceptions assumed identical based on appearance?
- **Hedging Fallacy** – Is the argument's meaning shifted in response to criticism?
- **Self-Sealing Fallacy** – Is the claim adjusted to make it irrefutable?

- **Weasel Words** – Are ambiguous terms used to make the argument sound stronger?

14. Is an Appeal Made to Personal Beliefs, Intuition, or Feelings?

- **Appeal to Personal Belief** – Is something claimed true because of one's belief or feeling?
- **Appeal to Intuition** – Is intuition used as evidence without objective reasoning?
- **Appeal to Nostalgia** – Is the past assumed better without supporting reasons?
- **Appeal to Novelty** – Is something assumed superior simply because it's new?

15. Are Specific Missteps Made in Cause and Effect Reasoning?

- **Post Hoc Fallacy** – Is a causal link assumed simply because one event followed another?
- **Confusing Necessary and Sufficient Conditions** – Is a necessary condition mistaken for a sufficient one, or vice versa?
- **Single Cause Fallacy** – Is an outcome oversimplified to one cause?
- **Self-Fulfilling Prophecy** – Is an outcome assumed true because actions made it so?

This checklist offers a structured approach to evaluating arguments and spotting common logical fallacies. With regular practice, you'll become more confident in identifying flawed reasoning and constructing strong, logical arguments of your own.

If you enjoyed this book, a review on Amazon would be greatly appreciated because it would mean a lot to hear from you.

To leave a review:

1. Open your camera app.
2. Point your mobile device at the QR code.
3. The review page will appear in your web browser.

Thanks for your support!

www.ingramcontent.com/pod-product-compliance
Lightning Source LLC
Chambersburg PA
CBHW061136120626
46546CB00005B/1809